LISA,
DONNA HAS BEEN TRAINING
ME FOR YEARS! - HAPPY 60th

I kissed my Frog.
He did not become a Prince.

My Frog kissed me.
I did not become a Princess.

Will we ever become Royalty?

ALL OUR LOVE,
RYAN
&
DONNA

HOW TO TRAIN YOUR HUSBAND
TO BECOME AN ADULT
(Humorous Tales to Enable Women
to Overcome Controlling Partners)

by Bernadine Fawcett

TABLE OF CONTENTS

PREFACE

This book does not apply to every man. For the men who read it and laugh, you know it was not meant for you. For the men who read it and become infuriated, you had better look at yourself carefully, because this book is about you. Read it and wherever you are the angriest with me the most, look at yourself and make some changes.

This book was not meant for every woman. The man in your life may be your worst enemy and his own worst enemy. If your relationship is violent, peruse it, enjoy it, but use utmost caution in applying any suggested solution within this book. Think through the consequences of any new devise before application, and that is good advice for everyone!

HOW TO TRAIN YOUR HUSBAND TO BECOME AN ADULT represents mythological and historical perspectives to identify and rectify immature behaviors and strategies. It satirically, ironically, paradoxically, and poignantly illustrates the humor of life. It exemplifies how to utilize humor to overcome and deflect disharmony. Enjoy!

INTRODUCTION

HOW TO TRAIN YOUR HUSBAND TO
BECOME AN ADULT

Humor heals. Humor motivates. Humor decreases tension. Humor deflects conflicts.

I attended a number of conferences which were devoted toward developing the incorporation of Humor into ones practice:

The Institute for The Advancement of Human Behavior in Atlanta Georgia and in Toronto Canada, Joel Goodman's The Humor Project conference in Saratoga Springs, New York. I've laughed with Annette Goodheart, PhD.,(Laughter Specialist) on stage in front of a large audience, listened to Bernie Siegel, M.D. author of LOVE, MEDICINE AND MIRACLES (et.al), Steve Allen, M.D. (Steve Allen's son), Steve Allen, himself, Peter Alsop, Ph.D.

folk-song-writer, and singer, Jean Houston Ph.D. who co-authored MIND GAMES (et al), Lynn Johnston FOR BETTER OR FOR WORSE cartoonist creator, and many more from the medical professionals themselves, who demonstrated that Humor heals.

Most of the forums included Norman Cousins self-experiments which illustrated and identified that slapstick comedy totally healed his serious illness.

As a practicing Marriage and Family Counselor since 1978, I've incorporated the humorous movement with a light touch of offered suggestions. This book reflects comical stories, one liners, and fairy tale analogies, that I frequently utilize. Laughter motivates as no other form of communication can. It is a permanent one-shot deal that makes the point, the giggling tickles the perception and clears the air, while an angry retort would stoke the fires and never accomplish harmony.

HOW TO TRAIN YOUR HUSBAND TO BECOME AN ADULT uproariously awakens the intellect to the history of immaturity; the strategies and upbringing practices that sustain it. It includes a detailed outline of how to utilize Humor to accomplish rewarding results.

After raising three successful children, I couldn't agree more heartily with Erik H. Erikson's premise that, as you train your children, they train you. As we raise our husbands, we raise ourselves. Women will obtain comic insights into their own behavior. The parent will identify with the developmental stages.

This book is meant to playfully envelop you into the serious subject of employing better family relationships, especially with your husband! A serious subject lightly handled for the comic-digestion.

Laugh! It's good for you.

Warning! Consult a professional before utilizing this book's suggestions if abusive relationships exist.

CHAPTER I
WHEN YOU WERE NOT LOOKING YOUR
HUSBAND TURNED INTO FROG

We awaken one morning and look over at the prince we've married. Low and behold! We are facing an ugly bullfrog. We gaze into the mirror and we have become the distorted frog-mates. A majority of marriages eventually reverse the fairy-tale of kissing the frog and he transforms into a prince. We kiss the prince and he mutates into a frog. Do the frogs kiss and everyone turns into a prince and princess again?

Well something like that. Certainly the next time your husband ungraciously embarrasses you in front of company, you might imagine that he is a frog that has just leaped into the punch bowl. As your guests replenish their drink, they are shocked by the frog sitting on the orange rind. He made a frog of himself. So laugh, instead of him laughing at you. That scenario helps to put his remark, which was out of place, in the proper place.

Our attitudes and imagery control our lives because we react to what we perceive the situation to be. We have to kiss the frog in order to convert him into a prince. Our mates have to kiss the frog to change us into their princess. The fairy tale is as difficult to create as it is to refashion reality. But what choice is left? Misery?

I'm going to kiss my frog. What are you going to do?

CHAPTER 2
FROGS OF THE WORLD UNITE

I have kissed the frog continually, but have I become one of the frog/women? Have I jumped into the water and swum with him? Have I caught his food for him, eaten it, and regurgitated it, so he wouldn't have to do the work of eating it himself? Then I wondered why my frog never became my prince.

I guess I have overlooked the fact that both of us frogs need to work at becoming a prince or princess. I think the fairy tale should be rewritten.

Here is my fairy tale:

In the beginning of history, there were only frogs. How could there be anything else? All the parents were frogs, so they gave birth to frogs. Frogs do nasty things. They loudly demand that the world be just the way they decree that it should be. Which would be fine, if all the frogs agreed on what those options should be, but each frog had a different concept of what their frog family should be.

Mrs. Equal Frog of one family felt that her husband should cooperate with family raising, finding food, and distributing it among the members. Her mate felt he did enough by warning all the predecessors away with loud belching noises at night which kept the family awake. After all, he

reasoned, that was what he was supposed to do, wasn't it? Another frog noticed that a neighboring family's male kindly helped his spouse. Mrs. E. was amazed that another neighbor, Mrs. Traditional was annoyed whenever her frog-mate attempted to catch a meal and share it with his family. The other Mrs. Traditional, felt the old ways of croaking all night were quite proper.

Something is terribly wrong, thought Mrs. Equal. Are we all deliberately trying to annoy our spouses? After much pondering she investigated the original family lifestyles. She discovered that generation after generation the frog's upbringing within the family unit seldom varied. The Equal frogs shared all duties and the Traditional frogs had an authoritarian base where the males were entitled to privileges that the females were outlawed from obtaining.

Mrs. Equal felt she had found some hidden truth. "Its easy," she said, "All I have to do is divorce my Traditional/type husband and find a family that lives the way I want, and I'll be happy."

So she divorced her beloved spouse and began to look for someone who had similar attitudes.

She became very discouraged and missed her husband; therefore she decided to seek him out.

Mr. Traditional/type was not available. He hadn't altered his attitudes. He merely found a companion who accepted his beliefs. Fashioned as a frog, he believed there was nothing wrong with his macho role image that he followed allowing him the privilege of belching all night. The crowd he hung with always belched all night, as their father's had. So what was wrong with that? Why should he change?

Mrs. Equal was very disappointed. She wanted a prince, but got a frog instead. Then she realized a crucial fact! She was a frog too!

Mrs. Equal began to take an inventory of her limitations and attributes. What did she need to do to become a princess? She decided to take some courses that would guide her. She was amazed to learn that it was a difficult process. She also learned that it was a myth that some prince would come along and kiss her and everything would be equalized! It hurt her to discover that she had to put years and years of effort into learning royal ways of kindness, understanding, independence, assertiveness and communication. She was so disappointed. She felt she would never reach her ideal goal.

Mrs. Equal learned to say no, and to present her objections in a firm, and gracious manner. She dealt with the guilt that other frogs tried to give her when she insisted upon her rights for a mature partnership. She kindly spoke her thoughts, her opinions, and her feelings, without threatening others with demands. She expressed herself without judging others. She waited graciously even though the other frogs misunderstood her actions. She tolerated the indiscretions of other's, knowing that she could not change them, discerning that they had to choose their own direction, that she could not foster it upon them.

One day Mrs. Equal looked down at her body and found that it was transformed. She had a beautiful gown on over a graceful body of a princess. She had made it! She had transformed herself. She was a princess. But her new frog mate was still a frog.

The moral of the fable is that we can only change ourselves, not anyone

else. However we could make the fable
go on:

Now that Mrs. Equal was a princess,
she tried to kiss her new frog-husband
to turn him into a prince. Of course, it
didn't work. Yet, something else
happened. her new husband began to
fall in love with the princess. He
decided he'd like to live in the castle
with her. He decided he needed to
change because he liked the renovated
partner. He started to see events
differently. He worked steadfastly
towards a mature ideal. He took on
responsibilities he had previously
shirked. He brought his tad poles to the
physician when they needed medical
care. He wrote his own thank you
notes. He even did household chores
without being reminded. Low and
behold! One day he found that he was
a prince. He courted the princess and
they continued to maintain the open-
communications between them so that
they wouldn't transform into frogs
again.

I like that Fairy tale because it's closer to reality. We are all frogs. We will become royalty only as long as we continue to work at diligently improving ourselves.

I wish that could be the end of the story, but all the couples' tadpoles, have already been exposed to the former misunderstandings and have incorporated them into their lifestyles without their young minds even being aware of what has happened.

Therefore as you read about the tadpoles: Sally, Mal, Tak, Al, Joe, John.etc., in the succeeding tales of the next generation which are struggling with many of the same issues as their parents. And so the cycle goes on.

Yet the new lineage is jumping out of the dirty water faster, and with greater grace. The happy thought is that the bullfrog is realizing his nightly soirees destroy his family's peace and harmony. He is seeking counseling now to learn the princely ways. The morale of the story is; improvement brings joy to everyone.

CHAPTER 3

FROGS AND OTHER THINGS

You don't want to hear a story about the drudgery of converting yourself from a frog to a princess. It's easier to hope for a fairy tale ending or some other type of magic formula. A fairy tale-book is a fantasy. Fantasies are magical if you know how to use them. The formula, is only as magical as you make it; with continual application, it does work if you try.

All marriages reach crossroads where one wonders if the marriage should continue or desist. As long as, an individual sits on the fence there is no commitment either way: to move out or to really work on the relationship.

What kind of fantasy would aid a decision? Imagine that you boarded an Ocean Liner without your spouse. Do you miss him? Do you want to return? What if you don't miss him? What if the freedom feels great? Could you start a new life elsewhere? What if you feel that you don't want to hurt him? Make believe that the ship sunk, but, by chance you washed ashore safely. However, your husband still thinks you are dead. Would you let him let him believe that you had not survived?

Let's imagine that you allowed him to grieve your demise. Then you found a job, then a furnished apartment. How do you feel as you walk into your own place for the first time?

Did you find utter loneliness without him? Or did you sigh with relief that you would never have to see him again? Perhaps the outcome of that imagery will motivate you to develop awareness of which choice you wish. The choice is yours. You need only make it. You may stay or leave depending on your selection based on your feelings.

A magic wand will not work as it does not have any control over your life. Nothing will change until you discover that your mind will free you, or trap you in an ivory tower. You have the power right between your ears. Use it.

Let's return to another version of the frog fairy tale:

Mr. Lazy Frog tells Mrs. L. that he is what he is, a frog; and he has no intention of changing himself into anything else. Her hubby demands that she live in the swamp while he floats in fresh clear water. She is trapped in the swamp until she begins to ponder. Then she wonders why she must be in the stagnant water while her spouse is in the clean water. So Mrs. L. hops into the clear water.

Mr. Lazy is enraged, "How dare you make yourself look so grand?" She began tittering. ending with convulsions of laughter; because she finally discerned that Mr. L. had always felt entitled to the fresh water. Only her self-diminishment had kept her from the enjoyment of it. Then he stated, "Ever since the beginning of time, female frogs have lived in the swamps, that's where females belong." Yet, she only swam away. Mr.. L. tried to catch her, but he couldn't.

The morale of the story is that there is never a solution until one envisions all the options available.

Disengagement is but one option. Other frogs stories end differently.

Mrs. Nagging Frog complains to Mr. N. about the nasty swamp water, "The water is too dirty. I can't get clean. It has leaves floating in it. The debris hurts my skin." She nags on and on expecting that she must wait for her spouse to alter her life condition; instead of taking the responsibility for her own situation. She could hop out of the water onto a cooling plant, but she waits for him to to give her permission. Mr. N. might buy her a life raft with which to float above the mess, but neither think of it. She will probably continue complaining: "The sun is too hot. The mud on my skin is cracking. My love for you is fading."

Mrs. Nag never specifies exactly what her requirements are so Mr. N has to guess what his next deed will be. She might have said, "I want you to clean up the debris." In that, it is what she desired.

Mr. Nag hoses her down. Mrs. N. sputters as water gets in her eyes, "You never do anything right!" Mr. N. says, "I can't read your mind," He really would like to please her. Since she never explicitly describes her needs; he tires of trying and leaves her for another female.

Mrs. Nag could have taken responsibility for her own life by jumping into the clear water with Mr. Nag and refuse to leave. She could have said, "I am equal with you. What's good for you - is

good for me. We have to have the same guidelines. I won't live any other way." Mrs. Nag could continue, "Of course, this is the way it should be! I love you. I want our life to be fair for both of us. I wish that you would say you love me, and then let's kiss and make up." Mr. Nag has to decide what guidelines he wishes to live by.

Mrs. Level-headed did specify her complaints. She let Mr. L-H. know that she didn't like the double guidelines for her and him. She said to him, "I feel like a second class frog. I feel abandoned and rejected. I love you very much and want to spend more time with you sharing the lovely cool clean water." Mr. L-H was very flattered. He invited Mrs. L-H. to join him in the lovely running water. They swam off together.

The morale of these stories is that everyone needs to specify what they want, define the situation, state their feelings and present the effect in a positive manner. Then, behave accordingly,

Now the fairy tale has a happy ending.

CHAPTER 4

SO NOW WHAT?

What do you do next? Assess your husband's level of maturation. Identifying that level helps to determine how to proceed.

Maturation is the independent acceptance of and perseverance of maintaining responsibilities. Yet, many males assume special prerogatives which allows them to neglect duties that they define by custom, as not male functions. The male mindset believes: he can do the activities he wishes because he is smarter, wiser, stronger; but mostly he's allowed because he has a penis. This gender-difference demarcates a cultural two level standard. The wife is supposed to be able to nurture, (which has come to mean, accept the husband's lack of willingness to share one half of the workload) keep house, be a lover, be a helpmate, and concentrate on the problems of housekeeping and child-raising. (All of these concepts include the traditional and the companionship roles for the male, but not the corresponding roles for the females.) Sometimes all these wifely duties are supposed to be simultaneously accomplished according to the male's perspective. (He says, "When are you going to put the toys away?" and then follows it with, "Hurry up so we can go to bed for some fun." as she is putting the laundry away after completing a full day of outside/paid employment.)

Woman would like to see a man run the house and make love simultaneously.

The independent wife might sweetly suggest: As soon as you show me how to do it dear, I'll gladly oblige you. Unfortunately, some women are uncomfortable being assertive. The husband demands empowerment , i.e., he has the right to make the rules.

He says: Stop what you are doing. Do what I want you to do, now.

His wife concedes to his attitude, his rules. The next morning she is confused by his anger that she should have somehow concurrently cleaned and made love. She feels guilty that she can't comply with his demands. She feels angry that she's caught in a catch 22 situation. She is dammed if she complies, and damned if she doesn't.

A playful husband may not differentiate juvenile tricks from humor. He laughs at a cruel joke he has played on his mate. This demeans her role as an adult. The confusion that she feels fosters a childlike clinging vine reaction in some women. The original Traditional role of our forefathers nurtured that dependent role. However, it does not fit today's society nor does it create a romantic response in the bedroom.

A woman must repeatedly identify herself as an adult. If this becomes a boring repetitious activity, then this is proof that the man you married is either trying to be your parent or your child. You need to make certain that you are neither his mother, nor his child. Handle the situations assertively. Repeat when necessary. "I am an adult. I am not one of your children. I will not be ordered around." Or state, "That's a childish prank; and as such, it is a put-down for not only my intelligence, but yours also." Or it may be necessary to say, "I will not tolerate living by two of sets of rules. Which set shall we eliminate?" If the male in your life can not live by the mature rules which you have made together, then it might be time for more stringent measures.

A woman may need to illustrate his obnoxious behavior by re-enacting or reiterating, his actions to him, while stating that you are dramatizing his behavior in order to enable him to view himself objectively. Ask him questions about his feelings. If he denies that he has feelings, ask, "Why does your tone of voice sound angry, if you aren't actually angry?" You might add a bear caricature, "It sounded like this: GRRR, GRRR." Slowly this might help him identify his emotions and actions. Most men have been indoctrinated to ignore their feelings. Since males hurt also, they need to maintain a protective shield that prevents them from responding to even their own emotions. Once that armor is in place, they are not aware of your anguish, nor their own. Slowly and gently women need to remove that armor with humor.

But first, it is important to know how this protective shield developed. Carl Rogers, an American clinical psychologist proposed the self-theory. The organism which is the total individual, is a composite of all the individuals experiences. The ego or self in which these experiences take shape determines the person's personality. An infant is told: "Don't cry. You're a big boy. Boy's don't cry." This perception does not integrate with the self that processes the hurt. The upset might have been a scrapped elbow or a sibling grabbing his toy. The infant/self must cry, thereby allowing a normal maturation of feelings or his total being may deny his own self- actualization. His reality is not conceptualized. He no longer-feels pain for himself, nor for others. If his life is studded with denial he may become more than immature in that one area of his life. He may be an incomplete personality.

Moreover accelerating maladjustment may develop into a complete inability to feel close to anyone. Lack of ability to internalize relationships causes various addictive problems (sexual and otherwise) according to Patrick Carnes, Ph.D. Luckily most men are only stalled in the playpen area in a minimal manner that becomes idiosyncratically sweet, although annoying.

Most of us are in this one huge play pen vying for the world's attention. So how is it that women get pulled into the playpen with their husbands? Erik

Erikson's premise is that adults generate satisfaction and a sense of accomplishment from life in order to integrate their own worth. So how can women command attention from a husband for emotional support when that source is dry? Women give nurturing until their well is drained. Who is left to replenish the water of life?

Below is a condensed version of the breakdown of the developmental stages for both sexes:

HUSBAND: I don't know what my wife is feeling or thinking, ever. I don't ask because I might find out something I don't want to hear. Then I'd have to deal with it. When she screams and carries on, I say nothing. I leave. Well sometimes I lie about where I went. I go to the races. I'm not having an affair or boozing it up. I'm a good husband. She can do whatever she wants. I don't stop her. The least she can do is live her life without bothering me. I can't understand why she wants to divorce me.

COUNSELOR: If you were looking for employment and didn't understand the job description, but took the job anyhow, then put no effort into finding out what was required of you; what would your employer do?

HUSBAND: He'd fire me.

COUNSELOR: Well your wife just fired you.

HUSBAND: What should I do? I don't want to put effort into the marriage just to have her leave me. She's left before and it hurts.

COUNSELOR: Would you require an employer who has found you to be an ineffectual employee, to give you a lifetime guarantee when you admittedly never gave the corporation any concerted effort to be loyal to their needs?

HUSBAND: I guess I messed up pretty good.

COUNSELOR: Your wife is emotionally drained from carrying the bride and groom's marital roles. However you are not totally to blame. You can only be blamed when you understand what has happened and still do nothing about it. Society has messed up. You are the fall out. We bring up our men and women to be incomplete individuals that are dependent on each other

to become a whole, and then step back and wonder why marriages, that require two adults to parent children and survive life; can't function.

If we are aware that we have an incomplete man then we should also be aware that many women are only one half of what they should be also. The female traditional role traits emphasize the mothering, dependent, clinging, naive qualities while punctuating the macho image. Each sex is one-half a person. Contrary to math where one half and one half makes a whole. Two halves in a traditional relationship equals less than half. This role ineffectually stumbles along in our present society. In relationship's math, two wholes are needed to establish one successful marriage.

If I've lost you, perhaps a life example will illustrate the the points that I am making:

Tony Incomplete and Margie Incomplete have a child. Joan, a pretty eight-year-old girl has Dad tucked into her pocket. Joan asks Dad, "Will you take me to Adventure-land?" Dad can't say no because he leaves the responsibility of refusing to his wife, even though he is aware they can't afford the excursion.

Margie is seething because Tony had told her, "All you do is spend, spend, spend. You think I enjoy working two jobs!" Now Margie thinks, 'Well you'll spend the money on Joan and not on me!' Margie's second thoughts are; 'How will we get the money to take Joan to Adventure-land? Now I'll have to be the one that has to listen to Joan's complaints when we don't go.' Somehow everyone will blame me for not going. Tony will say,' "Blame your Mom. If she hadn't bought that new dress, there would be enough money left for your fun."

Margie is left, as usual, to mend and enhance the familial relationships. She feels frustrated that she has to defend her expenses for her career which demands she maintain elite dress standards, while her spouse recently bought an expensive gun for recreational-hunting. Her daughter is too young to understand that clothes are a uniform which not only makes one feel good about oneself, but improves the job advancement possibilities.

That entire scenario arose from the male's basic insecurity The father couldn't say "no". What would his eight year old think of him if he did?

Margie couldn't verbalize her additional frustration of being made the family scapegoat goat who is not consulted in the decision making processes, especially the financial ones.

Is my premise of incomplete personalities correct? How complete are our personalities if we are looking for our children's approval rather than guiding them? Isn't that similar to a man pulling a donkey forward while hoping that the donkey's backward direction is the better way to go? Adults need mothering so badly that they must glean it from their child?

If we validate Rogerian self-theories then the uncompleted phase concept presented by this author gives us a handle on the situation. Margie might request that the entire family discuss the need for love for each individual. Margie, might mention to Joan, that not only does her Dad, but also, she, want to feel cared about.

That entire scenario arose from the male's basic insecurity The father couldn't say no. What would his eight year old think of him if he did?

Mom may reinforce her message by requesting that they all play a game together chosen by Joan in place of the outing.

Playful activities nurture both the offspring and the parents. Margie Incomplete got the family's attention by announcing, "Let's all stand on our heads! The world is upside down anyway. We can join the ranks with "ALICE IN WONDERLAND!"

Putting levity aside, Margie should request Tony's input on the best child-rearing goals, then ask for co-operative actions to reinforce these goals. This commences a peaceful, mature, home atmosphere. The situation is no longer out of control. Margie is acting as an adult, rather than becoming a co-dependent to an immature happenstance.

Parenting demands maturity from both Mr. and Mrs. Incomplete. Now their names could be changed to Mr. and Mrs. Complete.

CHAPTER 5
HUBBY DEMANDS ATTENTION

Yet, How can you state your feelings when you feel intimidated? Are you trapped and feeling helpless? Do you hesitate to state your real feeling, desires, or wants?

What are your reactions?

See which of the three below categories that you fit into:

1.

Business women are assertive and frequently have subliminally accepted concessions in the interests of peace. I am a business women. I, personally am told by my adult children that I'm extremely assertive. Yet, I, as a widow of thirty two years of marriage review with amazement how often I never thought to question my husband, Lyman's dictates. For example: He stated that we could not keep the kittens from our pet cat. I kept my emotional distance so that I wouldn't become attached. He played with them, then reversed his decision and encouraged them to sleep on our bed nightly for the span of sixteen years, much to my chagrin.

Lyman also determined our social life: the restaurants we went to, the board games we played, the activities that we shared. He merely passively resisted whenever I endeavored to make my determinations. The percentage of times in which we shared choices were less than one percent.

2.

Since these were not life threatening changes; I lived with it. Certainly each woman most vote according to the value of restriction verses the value of freedom. Is the marriage worth the loss of a minor infraction of freedom? If it is a major problem? You might ask yourself: Does it demean me so that I'm

losing my self esteem? Or have I
already lost It?

Some women accept the Traditional
role in which men are the major
decision makers. I wasn't aware, I, also
fell in this category. Frequently women
don't even realize they submit to men's
perceptions. The acceptance of male
authority from the outdated Traditional
roles, die hard. I know it took me years
to become aware of my automatic
acquiescence.

3. Other women nurture to the point of
not wanting to hurt their spouses
feelings, so they don't express their
dissatisfaction.

Women believe that if they set the
example, men will initiate the same
actions. Since many men don't accept
the nurturing role, the concept usually
doesn't work. Women need to express
themselves clearly, but this group is
unable to do it.

Therefore, as a marriage counselor
since 1978, I've reframed problems with

this fairy tale humor in mind, so that the situations are not so threatening.

The following analogies are meant to break through the female's conforming patterns. Utilizing these imageries facilitates ladies to lessen their fear, or reticence, so that they will have greater control over themselves by objectifying the menacing ways. They are not meant to be put-down humor and should not be used as such.

Try imagining your husband's behavior in the light of the age bracket that a child would act similarly in order that you no longer grant him the power to dominate you,.

For example:

The one-year-old-toddler will run from mom to explore the neighborhood, but screams when mommy leaves the house to go shopping without him.

Hubby will likewise ignore his wife if she is in the house, but will frantically call every friend his wife knows if she is out past 10 p.m.

Two-year-olds can be very demanding. They disallow mommy even the right to use the bathroom when nature calls.

Hubby leaves for work and is annoyed that his wife is on the john.

Three-year-olds pull at mom, while she is scrubbing the floor, doing the dishes or otherwise fully occupied, in order that mommy will admire the newest art scribbles.

Hubby does a home-project as he spouts nonsense, "What does a bee say to a pear blossom? I like you because you're sweet." The wife is preparing the evenings menu. The barrage of the husband's verbal stream of consciousness makes it difficult for her to concentrate.

The-four-year-old demands that mommy find his crayon he misplaced.

Hubby climbs the ladder to repair a picture and discovers he's forgotten the hammer. He calls his wife to hand him the hammer.

The-five-year-old is requested to wipe the dishes. His interest wanders and the dishes air dry.

Hubby is requested to bring up the completed wash from the cellar. The basket is still in the cellar, yet he can't understand why his clean socks aren't in his drawer.

The six-year-old wants mom to share Sesame Street in its entirety with him.

Hubby watches TV and voices his dissatisfaction when his mate reads a book. He chides her when she watches the soaps. He's disappointed when she hasn't the same excitement in a Yankee's game as he has.

The seven-year-old ignores mom's questions when he's totally engaged in his puzzle.

Hubby does not respond when his wife asks him if he has noticed the signs indicating a decrease in the speed limit. Driving the car in a racing mode takes his total concentration.

The eight-year-old insists mom, "look now!", at the way he bats the ball. Mother is making a soufflé.

Hubby insists his wife, "look now!", to see if she thinks the siding that he's nailed together, fits uniformly. She's balancing the monthly books.

The nine-year-old dons his Halloween mask and sneaks up behind mommy and yells, "boo!"

Hubby requests his wife climb the second ladder to help him hold the panelling to the ceiling as he staples one side. Then he climbs down from his ladder and gets a cup of coffee while his wife continues to hold the panelling. She can't let go or the panelling will rip out. He comes up behind her and yells "boo."

The ten-year-old stays after school to play ball without checking in with his mother. He can't understand why she is distraught when he finally arrives home. He knew where he was. So why was she worrying?

Hubby has a few drinks after work that lasts until the wee hours of the morning. He doesn't feel it necessary to let his wife know his whereabouts. He's fine and having a good time. He's certain his wife knows that also.

The eleven-year-old plays Monopoly with his friends. The game is unrecognizable because each want to reformulate the rules so they can win. Taunts of "you're cheating" break into fist fights.

Hubby has one set of rules for himself. He reads the newspaper when he visits his mother. Yet he informs his wife that she mustn't do needlepoint work there because it insults his mother with her seeming lack of concentration with his mother's conversation. However, he hasn't listened to one word his mother has said, as he reads his paper.

The twelve-year-old is very possessive of her toys. "Don't let anyone play with my Nintendo! Keep my brother out of my room!"

Hubby insists that even thought his wife rinses and changes the blade in his shaver that it ruins the razor whenever she uses it.

The thirteen-year-old liberally calls juvenile names such as: f--k you b-----h, and mother f ---- r, whenever angered by his playmates.

The deviant Traditional hubby will return his thwarted expectations with epithets similar to the adolescent.

The fourteen-year-old procrastinates until the moment for homework assignments.

Hubby puts off the painting projects for eight years and then is embittered that his spouse is angry when he finally gets to them. Or he says, "I'll do it, Honey," but never does accomplish the task.

The fifteen-year-old elaborately excuses his blunders. "I wasn't cheating. I was watching a fly zoom over my paper."

Hubby argues with his wife that it will be excess baggage to pack a jacket for a trip. The weather turns cold and he says, "Well how would I know that it would be cold in the mountains?"

The sixteen-year-old believes he's invincible. Car accidents happen to his friends, not him.

Hubby lets his toothache accelerate because denial has become a way of life. Ignore it. Maybe it will go away.

The seventeen-year-old is convinced that fast food is the best food in the world.

Hubby sniffs a gourmet meal his wife took days to prepare, and decides to visit McDonald's alone, yet.

The eighteen-year-old is certain he is old enough to make intelligent decisions about his future, and decides to work rather than go to college.

Whenever Hubby feels frustrated with his wife He says, "I won't eat supper. I'll have a piece of pie, instead,". (If you get suckered into worrying about his nutritional needs you are in big trouble. Now you're not just playing the role of daughter/employee, but you have also picked up the mother role.)

Hubby is an adult? I'll let you decide that.

Great grandmothers, grandmothers, and mothers have said, "Boys will be boys". A wife says, "My husband is my third child. The other two I gave birth to."

Age twenty-one is legal maturation. It depends on the criteria that we measure by: age, size, intellectual, or emotional maturation.

Women as well as men are often stuck at various levels of undeveloped maturation. They need to stand up for themselves.

The women of the world must unite! Bring up hubby from the infancy stages and bring up ourselves also. That is a difficult order but I think today's women are up to it.

How can we all make up for the love forfeited to a society in the middle of conflicting role/goals? Any child who is not allowed to scream (but in our culture it is usually mandated for males) when life is painful projects that agony. The resulting introversion causes dysfunctions such as an inability to relate emotionally to their spouses.

Being unable to express ones distress, dulls ones awareness. Men more frequently than women create a shield as strong as armor in order that they will no longer experience the ache. We all know that expression, "Take it like a man!" The result is an insensitivity to other people's emotions. It not only blocks negative emotions, but positive ones as well such as intimate-love. That type of cultural role creates a great deal of irretrievable love.

How can we love ourselves when we have never felt love? Imagine a room full of strangers who were hugging and kissing themselves. Absurd? Yes, but that is what we need to imagine ourselves doing. We beat ourselves up and each other with loads of guilt. Imagine the guilt as

if it were materialized as a wart. The room is full of folks with millions of warts covering their bodies. The warted people have all turned into frogs, leaping frantically in every direction looking for a way out of this guilt ridden room.

Is it a dream?

CHAPTER 6
THE FROGS LEAD US AGAIN

This Frog Fairy Tale suggests grown-ups set examples. After all, parents set standards for children. Then children expect their elders to live up to them. If adults do not, children see no reason to comply with what appears to them to be obviously capricious, and useless commands. Certainly the expectations are not important if parents are immature and doesn't feel the necessity to follow rules either! Therefore set an example for children or for your mate, which then sets the tone and mood for successful communication. Spouses and children automatically follow the lead person. Even our frogs found truth in that adage.

The second step is to allow your husband to take charge of his own life. It means freeing yourself of the responsibility of always being in control! Who has the problem? You or he? If it is his, let him solve it. If it is yours, solve it yourself. (Don't lean and don't command.) Securely take a stand and your husband will fall in place beside you.

Mrs. Equal Frog realized, she could only regulate herself. Her mate would have to come to terms with his own reality. Mrs. E. had seen many beautiful sunny days as she matured. Mrs. E. couldn't transpose her cheery nature upon her husband because he hadn't the fortune of experiencing happy times daily. She had immigrated from a happier part of the world. Life for him was one long cloudy day. Acclimatized to dissimilar occurrences he couldn't envision what had shaped her personality.

Each of us have experiences from life that lead us to different conclusions. We make assessments from those deductions. Since our experiences, are not identical we have different opinions. Therefore we need to discuss our differences, establish how they originated, in order to clarify our reasoning with each other, and then develop some guidelines that is acceptable to both parties. There needs to be a commitment to a mutual resolution so that life runs smoothly.

Flexibility is one of the most important traits needed to establish and maintain the vow that the couple has pledged to accomplish. It calls for acceptance of errors, supportiveness without suffocating the other with helpfulness, and allowing others the space to bear the consequences of their own behavior.

The couple needs to specify guidelines with each other, just as they outline rules for children. Mutual guidelines identify the situation and creates a comfort-zone because it gives specific directions for improvement. In the case of children we need to supervise or oversee. With adults we need to step back and allow the other to assume responsible behavior.

However, just as with the maturation process of children, the developmental stages should align with behavioral stages of growth: so should adult behavior be so aligned. The following additional tidbits (Yes! Another ages 1 through 21 child developmental cycle) which minimize the male all powerful entitlements by assigning them their rightful place.

The one-year-old is allowed to feed himself. Hubby should cut his own toenails. (However if it is a mutual aid system where each of you do it for the other, then we are speaking of equality in the best form).

The two-year-old is allowed to dress himself. Allow hubby to find his own clothes in the drawers and closets.

The three-year-old is allowed supervised freedom . Trust Hubby to not stray. Supervision doesn't apply here, because he isn't three years old, is he? A suspicious wife will only give the male justification for straying. If shackles and a leash is the sole method to prove faithfulness, then marriage becomes a haven or a halfway house? What would you prefer to have?

Deal with any straying behavior-decisively not with detective spying.

The four-year-old learns to pick up his toys after playing with them. Hubby leaves the cap off the tooth paste or his clothes wherever he took them off.

Hubby reacts best to positive messages, just as his son does. His wife's message could be, "When your shoes are left in the middle of the floor, it gives me the additional job of picking up after you. If the shoes are not noticed by me someone could fall and dislocate their back." If that message is ignored, the message can reiterate more dire results. A stronger suggestion might be adding some information such as, "Did you know that chiropractors best source of income comes from home-accidents?" If that brings no results a stronger statement such as "Did you know that most fatalities occur in the home? They are caused by careless actions of people who leave things laying about where others can stumble and fall." Make the information stronger and stronger until your husband finally chooses to pick up after himself.

Some men need to be shown what they are doing. If the above approaches are not helpful, try not returning his tools after you use them. When he becomes angry and berates you might try this scenario:

Wife smiles and says, "Now you know how I feel when you don't put things in their proper places." No doubt he will be perplexed.

Husband : What have my tools to do with my shoes?

Wife: When you want to find them, you know where to look.

Husband: I know where to look, wherever I left them last.

Wife: I am using these examples to illustrate to you exactly what you are doing. I'll leave your hammer wherever I stopped using it last. Of course I might forget where that was, since I don't use it often.

Hopefully, your mate will get the point that one should be responsible for ones own things and borrowed items. The key word is responsibility.

The-five-year-old brings home school assignments. Allow hubby the responsibility of setting and responding to his own alarm clock.

The six-year--old accomplishes homework assignments. Allow hubby to share the payments of debts and budgeting with you.

The seven-year-old is requested to cooperate by keeping his room clean. He learns to be a family member by this and other duties. Hubby leaves the bathroom in total disarray after his shower.

Specifying the necessity of drying the walls down after taking a shower because mildew forms. Mildew if left can invade the entire house and become a fatal health hazard. Supplying such information that you take for granted, but he hasn't considered, should bring more co-operation.

He really is oblivious to the family or house tasks unless your messages are precise.

He watched his father fix a car. You observed your mother as she cooked. Both genders learned from the experiences that society implied was their role. Do you know how to fix a car? In the majority of cases even Daddy's girls didn't notice the particulars of fixing a car. Well, most boys paid no attention to how to clean, cook, etc. as they followed Mom around.

The seven year child in your mate may respond to the vivacious message. "You like to play basketball. Why not try and see if you can make a basket as you throw your dirty clothes into the hamper?"

The eight-year-old is required to take out the garbage for his share of the household work.

Hubby must be informed that holiday preparations take several weeks of eight hour days to do the shopping, cleaning, cooking, serving, and cleanup afterwards. All of which is exhausting. The wife could provide a list of activities accompanied by an estimate of time that it takes to accomplish them and request he pick an equal time-share so that she won't be overburdened. Then everyone will be rested sufficiently to share a fun-filled party. She could state, "It is all work, just different kinds. I need your help."

The nine-year-old may visit his friends house alone. Hubby will most likely make a sigh of relief when his spouse suggests they both have breathing space of some time alone to pursue separate interests.

The ten-year-old is capable of watching his younger siblings while mother is putting on a wash.

Hubby can diaper and care for the children in his wife's absence, just as she does in his absence. His spouse can teach him these skills if they are lacking.

The eleven-year-old is expected to follow directions and complete his assignments.

Hubby can follow verbal directions of duties that the wife has not had time to finish. The wife may need to repeat, "I'm overwhelmed. I need your assistance."

The twelve-year-old should be capable of perseverance. Hubby should be capable of following the list without continual reminders in a marriage where both partners have full time outside employment. (Today most men do help and the ranks are growing. Hurrah!). Your husband is not your son, but your husband! Treat him that way. Don't rush in and assume his half of the household agenda or any other jobs that should be shared! I am recommending that as adults both should assume equal responsibilities and obligations. The gender label at places of employment is disappearing. Keep it on the move in your home.

The twelve year old has the brain of an adult without the experience of one. Hubby is an adult, but his experience with this new gender role is practically nil. He is trying to understand how to listen to his wife's emotions without blowing up.

The thirteen-year-old should be capable of mature logic. Hubby's threats of taking the car from his wife, when he is driving her car, can be met with logic. Reminding him that she could retaliate with the same action.

The fourteen-year-old should be able to concentrate. Hubby brings home the wrong brands from the supermarket list his wife prepared for him.

The fifteen-year-old should be trustworthy to follow his friends parent's house rules on overnight stays. Hubby should be able to drink without overindulging. His mate should allow the total repercussions of a DWI to be his. Step back and observe. Action is not needed here. The consequences arrive from the law.

The sixteen-year-old is allowed a juniors drivers license. The rules of the road are learned.

When hubby exceeds the speed limit, let him know that speeding with the family is unacceptable. That he needs to stop the car so that alternate transportation can be taken. Get out of the car and take the nearest taxi/bus/ train or airplane and meet him at your destination.

The seventeen-year-old is capable of using contraceptives if he is sexually active. When hubby acts surprised that his wife is pregnant and insinuates that it is not his, he needs to be informed that it took two to create this fetus. Both are equally liable for caution.

The eighteen-year-old may fight for our country. Hubby may take a life in war, and give a life in an adulterous affair, but he needs to be made aware that now he is required to contribute financially until that child reaches its legal-majority. The wife must reassess the marital vows if this transpires. Should she wish to remain married she must then decide what course of action is best when presented with her husband's out-of-wedlock child. Counseling can lessen the strain and decipher the best decisions for all involved-individuals. (Note that the wife has a choice and must determine her own selection of alternatives.)

The nineteen-year-old is allowed to date freely. The husband must be allowed respect, and the freedom to choose. Moreover, the wife has the same entitlements. These rights must be announced coherently by the wife. Church vows should be reviewed and agreed upon, if necessary.

The twenty-year-old goes to work, to college, and rents his own apartment. Hubby has the right to determine his life style, but then so does his mate.

The twenty-one-year old has all legal rights as an adult. Twenty-one is the age of legal majority.

Hubby has the right to judge his own behavior. and accept the consequences of it. The wife that doesn't interfere with that process, helps her husband to integrate his personality.

The options to all of these scenarios is the right to choose, but each has the privilege of their own boundaries. A wife's flexibility should not be tested to the limit. The woman should not wait until she is mentally or physically exhausted before taking action. A woman should take her courage in hand and make certain that her husband understands the requests that he has been ignoring.

Just as she would go for aid if her children were draining her energies, she should also find the best community resource to improve her marriage. Perhaps, if women identified the strategies of teenagers, it would establish a valuable assessment of immature behaviors. The next Chapter RING AROUND THE ROSY does that.

CHAPTER 7

RING AROUND THE ROSY

(Do Tad Poles create problems for the Bull Frog?)

Ring around the rosy
A pocket full of posy
Ashes-Ashes ------- We all fall down.

Just as nursery rhymes stay with us, so do the intuitive bargaining tactics of childhood which become refined in teenage years. These circumvention's appear to be the primitive (genetic?) side of us. Identifying the teenagers' strategies would establish a valuable assessment of immature behaviors. Women, also, adopt some of the thirteen teenage strategies listed here as well as men, but then we are not discussing women's foibles now, are we not? Moreover, since bringing up hubby is similar to raising children, then recognizing these strategies will benefit the couple. The following twelve game-plans are manipulations that I have identified as I have counseled teenagers.

THE THIRTEEN TEENAGE STRATEGIES

I. AUTHORITY OVER YOU

Definition: The child cites a type of authority over his parents. The child will assert that his teacher said he had to have a computer immediately or he'll be thrown out of school. Children's outrageous use of authority may be seen through easily, but a male adult's use of authority is perceived more as a threat:

Mrs. Y.. tells her husband that tomorrow while he is at work she is going to visit her parent's home nearby.

Mr. Y. : You can't go.

Mrs.: Why?

Mr. Y : The weather is going to be bad, the roads will be slick.

Mrs. Y : I'll decide tomorrow by what the roads look like.

Mr. Y: No I want you home when I come home. I want you to make me home-made chicken soup.

Mrs. Y: I'll open a can.

Mr. Y: My mother always made me chicken soup when I had a cold.

Mrs. Y: Nobody makes soup today.

Mr. Y: My parents were a Traditional couple. What was good enough for them is good enough for me.

Mrs. Y: The day you wear your hair in Hasidic curls I'll comply.

Notice that when the husband's authority was questioned, the male then used his mother, and then the Traditional roles that dictated the wife's compliance. The wife stretched absurdity to provoke consideration of her viewpoints from her husband's use of the Classical Traditional Role in an attempt to confront the two types of authority that her husband is using to keep her in line.

II. WEAR YOU DOWN

Definition: When women use this technique it's considered nagging. Coming from a child, it would be labelled whining. From a man, it's thought of as orders. It's the continual repetition of a need, message, or desire voiced as a command rather than verbalized as a matter of fact.

This male's purpose is to secure more sex for his needs. He states:

On night one: You used to wear flimsy-black negligees to bed.

Night two: You used to be more athletic in bed.

Night three: You used to want me more than once a week.

Night four: You used to be the aggressor.

Night five: You used to wear enticing perfume.

Night six: You used to shower every evening. Now you shower in the morning.

Night seven: You lost the excitement of our honeymoon.

This frustrated wife finally responds with scalding humor (which is not recommended), "God made the world in seven days. In seven nights you couldn't make it once."

Although the nasty approach alerted the males attention from his continual threatening "you messages". Her message was a "you" message also. "You" messages accuse and threaten.

"I" messages don't threaten. They state your feelings. The little lady may ask for a truce of "I" messages. She might say, "I would also like to enjoy our lovemaking as we did on our honeymoon. How can we make it better?" She might say, "Why don't you say to me?, 'I would love to see you in a flimsy-black negligee.' or- 'I bought you this new one,' or 'Let's take a shower together and soap each other down."' These are clear, concise messages that points the partner in the right direction.

Probably he'll respond positively. He might counter the female's remarks with "You are over sensitive," etc.

The wife can respond: "Your remarks were judgmental."

Stating that your preference is your opinion or feeling which is acceptable as long as you frame it as such.

Stick to your guns! If the woman accepts the husbands third person pronoun remarks of "you" as a command, then she feels forced to passively resist his demands and the relationship becomes more strained. (Females often withdraw sexually, or forget to run an errand that is important to him, etc.).

Instead, the woman might try to get her husband to read this book. (If he reads it, ask him to identify which type of marital role(s) agrees with his expectations.) The wife should evaluate her own expectations. Then, she could determine what causes the conflicts. Next they might work toward solving the recognizable problems.

If ones mate refuses to participate, the wife might suggest that he tell her what bothers him using the pronoun "I" because she feels as he is acting as if he were her father when he uses the third person pronoun, "you". She might add with a coy flair: "It's incestuous to have sex with your father. Consider what I'm saying because your communication skills are adversely effecting our sex life."

The tone of voice that a woman uses to express herself is as important as the male's. A non- accusatory inflection is extremely important along with retaining your wit!

III. MAKE YOU FEEL GUILTY

Definition: A statement that is meant to try and make you feel guilty. The person or child delivering this remark understands how you think and deliberately attempts to reproach you for manipulative reasons. The youth states, "All the other kids have one. Why won't you get me a baseball suit?"

The reader has probably noticed the blame is used in the above examples along with each maneuver. The reader will notice that all of the thirteen techniques may mix and match into a combined forceful whole in order to obtain dominance over the situation.

The below remarks made to a woman that prides herself in keeping an immaculate home and her rebuttals to deflect the fault that her spouse is directing towards her:

Husband: The top of the refrigerator is dusty. How can you think of joining your friends for coffee

Wife: Why? Are you lonely?

Husband: The dishes are still in the sink. There won't be time to go to the movies tonight. (A statement that appears to be factual, but is threatening because it is obviously unnecessary. This type of wife wouldn't leave the house without everything being in its place and he is well aware of it. However he is taking a supervisory position that implies the work wouldn't be completed without his comments.)

Wife: (Make remarks in jest. It should not be barbed. Instead, assume more of an invitational remark.) Then you're planning a coup de deux for us instead of snoozing?

Husband ignoring the remark that is too accurate. He continues the attack: "I can't see out of the windows. While you do them, I'll just watch the Super-bowl game. "

Wife: "That's balanced. You enjoy life and I work."

A woman could become a stand-up comic as she establishes the real issues which are behind the guilt comments that the husband is attempting to load on her. Frequently bantering allows the man to burst out laughing, accept his foibles in order to make subtle changes without a losing face.

There is an attempt of controlling her daily-actions that harps back to Authority Over You. The wife in the above examples refuses to allow the husband to influence her. Instead she draws attention to the remarks in a farcical manner. Her next step would be to draw out the reasons for her spouse attitude to maintain power over her.

The best way to avoid a power struggle, is to ignore the attempts at maintaining jurisdiction, by side-stepping them, creating humorous interplays and then continuing ones activities as if the power-play never existed. The woman restructures the comment so that the discussion will feature the real desires of the male.

Moreover, she is announcing her options to enjoy herself which is otherwise restricted by his constant inattentiveness or sleeping. First determine the cause. Is it a step disorder? Working long hours? Or is it withdrawal from conflict? If the last option is determined, the wife might state her intentions: "I will stay home if there is some promise of a more interesting happening between us."

His opposition has been to refuse to confront the problem, (The male has used the female pejorative here. It doesn't work well does it?) and then use an employers stance of establishing work goals for her. Some males establish one obstacle after another expecting the mate to hurtle over them in order to feed his ever needy ego. Females need not accept this exploitation. Instead this woman airily kisses her mate, tells him to enjoy himself as she announces that she will spend the Super-bowl afternoon viewing a movie she always wanted to see.

For the successful woman who alters the strategies, she will also alter the Classical Traditional Role towards a less Blinded Traditional type. A woman that accepts these child-evasions and does his bidding has accepted his control over her actions.

IV. TELLS YOU, "I HATE YOU."

Definition: Manipulation of your emotions to gain controll over your actions. Children instinctively know that the parents really love them. They hurt parents to the quick, by flinging: "I hate you!" remarks. The teen engineers the parent into attempting to win back the juvenile's affection. If the parent falls for this intrigue, then the teen is in control again. However, marriages are more frail, because the wife does not automatically assume that her mate is just trying to control her when he announces that he despises her. She believes him. He may even have convinced himself that he wants a divorce. The wife personalizes the negative comments and often guiltily tries to rectify the husband's version of the situation.

Mr. Q. refuses to discuss why he arrived home one hour late. Instead, after fifteen minutes of silence he explodes, "I want a divorce. I hate you. I never loved you, anyhow." He is threatened by what he perceives is a power play to win back the top position.

Mrs. Q. has noticed that Mr. Q. frequently unlashes a virulent attack when she questions his actions. Mr. Q. often commences a normal discussion as if nothing happened a few minutes after his outburst. On this occasion, Mrs. Q. is prepared. She hands Mr. Q. a prepared official looking document that reads:

Mrs. Q. vs. Mr. Q. in court action:

SWIFT DIVORCES MADE EASY; DIVORCE INGREDIENTS:

THREE DECLARATIONS OF HATE.

THREE DECLARATIONS OF NEVER HAVING LOVED ONES SPOUSE.

ONE DECLARATION OF DESIRE FOR DIVORCE.

MIX ALL OF THE ABOVE WITH AN ANGRY TONE OF VOICE AND ONE DIVORCE COMING UP!

Mrs. Q. has quietly demarcated her decisions. If Mr. Q. ignores the whimsical warning, Mrs. Q. follows through on her swift divorce. It is imperative that one consider the ramifications of any action before taking it. Nevertheless unless you are determined to follow through on your commitment to maintain your sense of self, you will lose it. It has been my experience when working with couples, that after the male totally chisels the wife into this wimpy automat he loses interest in the marriage.

Mrs. Q. has shown her diplomatic resolve to maintain logical behavior when faced with emotional reactions and has made Mr. Q. aware that she's aware he's playing a game.

An objective view is needed to determine a resolution to the conflict.

When your ten year old child changes the rules because he's losing, you make him aware that the new rules are now enforced for everyone The same guidelines apply to marriage. Play by the new set of standards with the expectation all will honor the guidelines equally. Hubby can be coyly warned.

If he takes offense, be cautious. He has a sense of entitlement that may be a barometer of mental illness and not ignorance of the new cultural standards of equality. A Self-help book should never take the place of counseling, but should be used in conjunction with it, especially in borderline cases when you have any reservations.

V. IGNORE YOU AND MUTUAL GUIDELINES.

Definition: Withdrawal from any emotionally charged issue.

Adolescents ignore the rules to do household chores. Teens make believe that they didn't hear the curfew hour set for them.

Some males refuse acknowledgement of mutual guidelines or ignore those already established. Then they exploit this scheme to their own advantage.

There is a cultural presumption (apparently shared predominately by the feminine side) that marriage is a commitment of a lifetime of romantic love. Some men seem to lose sight of that as soon as the vows are said.

Therefore, when a lady expresses a desire to have the gentleman verbally declare his love more than the one time other than his proposal; and the husband says, "I wouldn't have married you if I didn't love you. Why do you need a constant declaration?" The wife feels his reticence is proof that he no longer cares for her.

Here's an inflated situation, but you'll get the idea with this ludicrous example:

The disappointed wife approaches a gravestone engraver and orders a stone. When the stone is delivered to the house, she places it prominently in the living room. When her husband returns home, he asks, "Why is this gravestone standing in our living room?" The wife says, "It's the only assurance I'll get. I'll have to settle for this daily reminder.'" The tombstone reads: I love you. Your loving husband.

Needless to say this husband now prefers to profess daily verbal proclamations of romance. The wife obtained his attention. His laughter was caused by relief that the gravestone wasn't a sign that she wised him dead. He realized that her message was that if he didn't openly profess his love, her love might die. His wife had reverted to a subliminal message because her open communication wasn't reaching his heart. The stone was put aside for the distant future's use. The goal was accomplished.

The couple mutually agreed to go out at least once a week. It could be a picnic, movie, having friends over, eating out, dancing or whatever enjoyed by both. Inexpensive times could be interspersed with luxury times according to their economic situation.

The verbal agreement of the couple was disregarded. The husband continued to refuse to accept her company, in his home, or out, or take his wife to any function. The non-conformance must be re-addressed. He sleeps, watches TV, and pursues his hobbies as if he were living a bachelor's existence. The wife, then, has become disillusioned as her frequent and loud complaints are ignored.

A concerned woman friend gives this DECLARATION OF INDEPENDENCE paper to the wife to give to her husband. It states:

DECLARATION OF INDEPENDENCE

I hereby secede from this marriage until such time as it is unified to perform a concerted effort toward happiness.

I will act independently to find happiness. Those goals will be done within the confines of the marriage contract but, with no other restrictions, due to this already one sided marriage.

This DECLARATION OF INDEPENDENCE will be withdrawn should you wish to become a participating member in the pursuit of happiness.

The wife decided to pass it on to her husband, because she had used every method she knew, to no avail. Perhaps her husband will be awakened by this fanciful approach that states her real intentions. Breaking through the preoccupation of unmindful males, sometimes necessitates extreme projects to obtain their attention. He wanted to know if she meant it. She said she did not desire it, but she would follow through if things didn't improve. The relationship improved because he realized that her whimsy was of serious intent.

In this example:

The husband had agreed to share the workload of a two-wage earner family by food-shopping weekly and cooking three nights a week. However no food has entered the house via the husband since that agreement, nor will he acknowledge a specific schedule of the nights he agreed to cook. The wife has expressed her disappointment that he is not co-operating. She has told him she is overwhelmed and exhausted by the overload of work. He has not complied and it has been a month since her initial protest, but the duties remain unshared.

The wife wishes to handle the situation with as much attention-getting-whimsical-creativity as possible since communication skills are not reaching his motivational level.

Therefore, the next time the wife shops, she buys a month's worth of dried beans of all varieties, and fresh vegetables of all descriptions. She then prepares and freezes several months of soups, utilizing the beans as protein stock and the vegetables for the extra nutrients needed for healthful eating. Next she thaws one batch of soup and serves it one evening after another.

When her husband complains of the gaseous components and boring dinners, his wife remarks: "I haven't the time to prepare fancy dishes. I haven't had a relief of duty so I've had to find a way to provide a healthy diet with minimal effort."

She gave him a forceful, innovative, verbal message and left the decision to her husband.

In the above case the man felt unequal to prepare food and bargained with time management to allow him to complete household obligations of scrubbing floors and toilets, and vacuuming. Whenever he forgot his wife reverted to the soup route. She tells me that he hasn't forgotten for several years now after the second treatment that propelled her husband into participating.

Provocative solutions will help motivate action from the TV-couch-bleacher.

VI. DISTRACT YOU

Definition: When you ask a child to do something or speak to them about something they shouldn't be doing: they will knock something over, antagonize a younger sibling or divert your interest in any way that they can. Men adopt comparable tactics.

Stella asks Harry to mow the lawn. Harry develops instant deafness. He discards what Stella has said. He relates a joke that Pete told him at work. She temporarily forgets her request. Harry returns to his hobby.

Jake gets his fifth beer in one hour from the refrigerator, downs it in seconds as he sits in front of the TV ball game. Julie inquires as to how many drinks he's had. Jake smiles, and pats her rear perfunctorily three times without answering her questions.

Julie can't obtain Jake's immediate co-operation.

Julie has a large problem since Jake is an alcoholic. She washed out every can that Jake drank and kept them. At first Jake was unaware that Julie was accumulating beer cans, until he opened a closet and they all fell on him. Jake demanded that Julie throw them away. However, Julie insisted that as long as Jake drank, that she would amuse herself with stacking his beer cans. In a rather short time the living room looked more like the local dump and still Julie refused to throw them out. At no time, did Julie request Jake to stop drinking. Jake's drinking became very evident to him since he had to face the growing mound of empty cans. He stopped drinking. Of course not everyone would react as Jake did. Some men would buy another house to store the cans.

VII. MERRY-GO-ROUND

Definition: This is an additional ploy to Distract You except the distraction is accomplished by changing the focus of discussion. Teenagers will show you their poor report card. While you are scolding them for the bad marks, they might divert your attention by spilling coke on the living room rug. This will discharge the anger in two places and might even create enough confusion so that the parent forgets the report card. If the parent remembers the report card incident, the teen is prepared to argue whatever subject he can engage the parents with that is the furthest removed from educational accomplishments. The youth accomplishes all this

through conversation and antagonistic questions whenever the parent returns to the original topic.

Although both sexes can be equally adept at this, let me again remind my reader that I am discussing only the male's adaptation to this technique.

Joy: Where is the milk I asked you to bring home.

Joe: (Grabs Joy and kisses her.)

Joy: (Decides that Joe is trying to distract her so she becomes angry.) Please go out and get the milk. I need it for my cooking.

Joe: Did you make pizza tonight?

Joy: I didn't have time.

Joe: You promised you'd make me pizza

Joy: I don't have the time tonight to do it. Will you please go to the store for milk?

Joe: When you didn't bother to make me pizza? By the way, the slipcovers aren't on the sofa.

Joy: When am I supposed to have time to accomplish everything? The baby has been sick all day. I've had to-

Joe: (Interrupting) Did you call the doctor?

Joy: She just has a virus. It will pass.

Joe: Bart told me a joke today. Two men were fishing-

Joy: (Interrupting) I've got a bigger joke. No milk, no dinner.

Joe: What do you need milk for?

Joy: The cheese sauce for the macaroni.

Joe: I'd better check the baby.

Joy: Let the baby sleep. Please get me some milk so I can complete dinner.

Joe: Did you hear the News today?

Joy: (Laughingly uttered) Flash! Joe did not get his pizza-nor his macaroni and cheese.

Joy kept the focus on the needed milk. Therefore, she foiled Joe's roundabout discourse. Both genders should be aware of what contributes to the whirligig momentum. Joy could have become side tracked, instead she continued to assert the goal and then humorously pointed out the results of non-compliance, Therefore, Joy prevented the carousel from spinning on. Foiled in all his attempts at distraction, Joe left to purchase the milk.

More of the Merry-Go-Round technique:

David has had many one night stands. He finds them challenging and invigorating. David does not want his wife to know about his mistress. He is trying to create more unquestioned time for himself so that he may dally at will.

Carol, his wife questions: Where were you until 3:00 a.m.?

David: I know where I was. Where were you?

Carol: What do you mean? I was home.

David: Well since I wasn't here to prove you were home, how do I know that to be true?

(He attacks to put her on the defensive.)

Carol: I was home all night. Ask the children.

David: Did the children stay awake all night? If they did, what kind of a mother are you? To allow the kids to be up to keep you company.

Carol: I'm a good mother. You know it!

David: You need to discipline them better. They are spoilt.

For the time being David has used the carousel technique at its utmost effectiveness. He has directed the attack from his late-arriving hour to an attack upon the way that Carol disciplines the children.

A replay of this circular technique with Carol halting the carousel follows:

Carol : Where were you until 3:00 a.m.?

David: I know where I was. Where were you?

Carol is already becoming aware of the roundabout affront, "I was here. If I weren't, how would I know what time you got in?"

David is still trying the manipulative technique, "Well you were here when I got in. How do I know you weren't here and then returned before I?"

Carol is very aware of David's offensive moves. She feels in control of the situation, because she knows what to expect next. "Well you better get home early to check on me! You never can tell what the mouse will do when the cat is away."

David: Are you telling me I should be worried about you? Who are you seeing?

Carol: I asked first. I'll answer all questions after you tell me who you're seeing.

Note that Carol has playfully maneuvered David back to the objective of her first inquiry. As long as she maintains the focus on the issue, she will accomplish her aim of getting the information she wishes. Then it is up to both parties to resolve the crisis.

The merry-go-round technique is employed in minor priority circumstances such as:

Mrs. Neat requests: Could you put your socks in the hamper? It is only one foot away from you."

Mr. N. responds with an unrelated attack: You have a fetish about neatness. I like my pliers to be in the kitchen drawer so that I don't have to climb up and down the stairs to get it, but will you leave them there? Oh no! You have to put them in the cellar so that it takes me longer to accomplish my jobs.

Mrs. Neat : Everything has a place, and everything in its place. Then you can find it.

Mr. N. still attacking to cover up his lack of conformity: I call it compulsive behaviors.

Mrs. Neat is taking the bait and defending herself: I'm not compulsive. I'm organized.

Mr. N.: You cleaned my tools with soap and water. They're all rusted now. Did you think they would dry like dishes?

He is on firmer ground now because he's remembered a more serious faux pas.

Mr. N: That was stupid of me. I wasn't thinking. I meant to help you. (Admit a clear mistake so that the manipulation ends for this issue.)

Mr. N. is now on a roll He tries a new attack: With that kind of help, we'll go broke in a year. Which reminds me, how much did that pink dress cost? We're not millionaires you know.

Mrs. Neat is now defending herself in the area of finances. Her husband can breathe freely because the attack is no longer directed towards him, but towards her. It is a circuitous movement to divert attention away from any issue that he is unwilling to change, and towards any issue that accomplishes this objective to assure that the subject will not be broached for the duration of the dispute. He even wins points because he is gaining control over his wife's financial decisions.

Again note that the method is to change the subject by attack or misdirection as quickly as possible. Usually the circular reaction continues on as long as is needed. It often escalates from fencing over trivial matters into major disputes. Both spouses view it as a matter of integrity to control their own space, and attempt to do that by trying to control the other partner's space.

Without having to control anything except ones own actions, Mrs. Neat might have utilized her awareness of the circus atmosphere by preventing it to continue in this manner:

Mrs. Neat: I'd appreciate your putting your socks in the hamper. My back aches when I have to pick up after so many people in the family.

Mr. N.: If you'd teach the kids to help you. You wouldn't have to do it.

Mrs. Neat is aware of the technique beginning again: There are two things I need accomplished. The socks picked up, and less stress for my back. Since they're your socks, I'll let you solve how they get picked up. You can use a fork lift if you want, but the socks will lay there unwashed unless they make it into the hamper.

Mr. N. doesn't give up easily: Call the kids to do it.

Mr. N: You call the kids. They're your socks. It's your problem. Don't expect me to solve it for you.

Mr. N.: You're the mother. You're supposed to discipline the kids.

Mrs.. Neat does not involve herself in this diversionary rebuttal. (She uses repetition of her statement until he complies in order to extinguish his manipulation): I'm interested in one thing only, and that is-the socks should be removed from the floor into the proper storage container. I will discuss the children's actions as soon as you cooperate.

Many women will find that husbands that use this merry-go-round technique do not quit. They have the tenacity of a Saddam Hussein. They bunker down and bombing raids brings on sideline attacks. Therefore, the women must be prepared to stick to their goal, redirecting the male to the issue until it is resolved. For this reason humor is suggested because it decreases the tensions and zeros in precisely on the behavior that is objectionable.

For example, the wife might say: I notice your socks have leaped to the floor. I wonder if they could hop-skip the rest of the way into the hamper?

Unfortunately, any confrontation is offensive to a woman who feels that assertiveness typifies unwomanly behavior. Further discussion about the timidity of women to stand their ground (they need to realize being assertive is ladylike.) This issue is handled at great length in Chapters 8, 15, and 21.

The Merry-go-Round technique is the most frequently used method, to divert attention by all members of the human race and therefore it pays dividends to be totally aware of an analysis of this strategy.

(A.) Divert attention verbally by discussions, verbal assaults or by creating a derisive action.

(B.) Maintaining the diversionary expressions as long, and as often as they are needed to keep the spouse/parent off balance so that the targeted person does not achieve the desired end result.

Once you are expertly familiar with this method, you can sit back and watch how cleverly the game is played. It is analogous to a chess game with moves and counter moves. I labelled it the Merry-Go-Round because it leads nowhere. It is not meant to be directive. It is only meant to lead one in circles. It reminds me of my cat who chases her tail. However, from time to time, even she see this as fruitless activity. Therefore she sits squarely on her butt with her tail caught between her legs and then she precedes to groom it-as was her intent. Wives need to squarely approach their issues with the same cognitive tenacity.

VIII. ASSUME CONTROL

Definition: This is one advanced step over the method of Authority Over You.

It is no longer a verbal directive, but a behavior-that is assuming control by vanquish. The teen might stay out all night and belligerently defy your authority to maintain curfews. The male might use this technique by assuming whatever he decides should be accomplished without a mutual agreement. He might close out bank accounts. He might command the children, overriding his wife's directives. insidious method is difficult to discern because a fait-accompli tends to create a defeatist attitude for the target person.

This type of control demands all the creativity one can command to attempt to break through a stronghold that strangles the independence of another person. Control issues are on a continuum from verbally mild to the extremes of violence that is fatal.

Should the reins tighten, there is always the option to pack your bags and leave. (If the male becomes increasingly restrictive; the wife should be cautious because this profile lends itself towards violence.) You have the option to leave anytime your want. There are no chains on your ankles. There may be chains on your heart. There is no one else but you to decide whether the pain you're enduring is worth sustaining the relationship. Make a list of the pros and cons of his qualities, traits, and morals. Then make your decision based on your test. If the score is negative, but you can't or won't tear yourself away from him, while you live with him; work on the relationship. Obtain his co-operation with amusing approaches in order to involve him in the relationship-process. Life improves more rapidly when two work at the marital difficulties together.

An immature male is potentially dangerous because his infantile thinking is encased in jan adult male body that has the potential to inflict harm from minor abrasions escalating to murder. This book does not suggest any methods for these abusive situations, other than to seek counseling and escape to a halfway house for protection. Again, extreme caution is advised when determining the women's availability of choices when dealing with deviant males. WARNING: Humorous solutions may inflame an already dangerous situation. Assess your lifestyle before applying any method that might inflame a man whose coping skills are undeveloped. If you have any doubts as to a course of action, check with a professional counselor. All self-help books are limited to the subject matter and can not give personal attention to each and every situation.

If a woman does not know how to evaluate her situation; here are some guidelines that will aid a woman to determine whether she has only an attitudinal immature individual or one that is deviant. (Also refer to the Chapters 18, 19, and 20, which gives further details on the Deviant Traditional Role.

Do not confront aberrant behavior such as those listed below. Seek professional help.

Any pushing, shoving, slapping, squeezing, throwing things, or holding one down should be viewed as potentially dangerous. These actions may accelerate into full-violence that require hospitalization or a casket.

Control over your use of the telephone, how often or when you visit with your friends.

Control over your resources such as money, use of a car, etc.

Use of obscene language or overt put-downs.

Beware of a honeymoon period after the violence.

Any of the above behaviors should be viewed with caution: Especially if the minor infractions do not immediately cease.

Insistence on any activity at his convenience whether it is sex, housework, or outside socializing.

The abusive behaviors are repeated after they are brought to the attention of the aggressor. A second incident, even if followed years latter should still be considered dangerous to ones health.

There are those males who would never become violent but, they still violate the rights of the female by denying her freedom. There is justification for insisting on counseling or psychiatric evaluation. If the wife abuses a freedom such as consistently overcharging on credit cards, causing debts beyond the incoming finances, then the husband might have to take over the management of the accounts, but only until such time as his wife rectifies her habits The use of control is legitimate only when it is to save the family from bankruptcy proceedings, because his wife is immature; instead of his being immature. You see? I am not a husband basher. There should be equality on both sides for both spouses. Equality demands responsible, stable, mature behavior or the process breaks down. However, this material assumes that the wife performs responsibly. If you are not mature (i.e. having an affair, abusive language, etc.), seek help.

Many young people who marry as teenagers, treat each other, as they did as siblings within their family, or the classmates at school, with verbal or physical fights. The husband may believe he is not exerting force, nor controlling because he feels it's his role based on his view of macho Traditional concepts that are still lingering in our schools. I speak with many school teachers and the Traditional role is alive and kicking in the high schools on Long Island! Unfortunately these immature patterns remain-often for years.

Let's assume that you have correctly determined that your husband's control is not the lethal variety but simply a misunderstanding of what his role should be.

For example:

Sam says as he takes the phone from his wife: Put the phone down. I'm home now.

Betty belly flops on the floor and salamanders backwards: Oh! Royal King of Siam, your every wish is my command!

Note that the extremist form of absurd-humor is needed to break the tension, delineate and pin point attention to the issue. The idea is to create such a shock from reality that the spouse alters his view of controlling behaviors.

How to use Humor to reverse and diffuse situations is dealt with at greater length in the Chapter 26.

Tom says to his wife's friends: It's time to go home now.

His wife says with a confident smile on her face: I'll go with my friends. (as she walks out the door).

Tom says: Stay here!

Wife: "Ask us all back and I'll return."

The directive may be instead an unspoken assumption that the wife fulfills because the wife hasn't questioned the patterned behavior that their families of origin enacted.

For example:

Matthew says without any forethought: We're going camping this weekend. Bring the equipment up from the cellar. His wife, Eve follows his directive without questions.

Eve wants to go on a picnic. The following weekend she prepares the food, but Matthew refuses to go. She becomes aware that Matthew's taking-control-approach does not apply to her; because Matthew's compliance does not match hers. She begins to understand that there are two sets of rules: his and hers. His rules are complied with, hers are not.

The next time Matthew states that Eve prepare for an activity he decides without mutual agreement, Eve does nothing. When Matthew is perplexed and vexed over her non- compliance, Eve explains the picnic situation; her reasoning of the situation and her conclusions, being careful to not allow her action to be viewed as a revengeful action: but, instead suggesting that co-operative and mutual decisions that encompass activities and work responsibilities be shared.

Continued example of the above situation:

Matthew: Get the camping equipment from the cellar, We'll stay at the beach overnight, tonight.

Eve: You can lug up whatever you want for your own use. I am not going.

Matthew: Why?

Eve: Players on a team, all use the same rules. I cooperated with you to go camping, but you won't go on a picnic with me.

Matthew: What are you talking about? We all go camping together.

Eve: But you won't go to the picnic.

Matthew: I don't like picnics.

Eve: I don't like camping. By your rule s if you don't like to do something, you don't do it. I'm playing by your rules.

Eve pointed out the basic inadequacies of the marriage. Now the stage is set for the couple to re-negotiate a viable solution where everyone is happy.

Another technique for harmony is a type of bartering stances. One spouse will participate without great pleasure so that the other spouse may enjoy him or herself. Barter, something that you enjoy doing for something that you don't. Then the next time he does something he doesn't care for-for something that you like.

John likes to go boating. Mary does not, but she goes with a pleasant attitude. Mary likes to shop. John does not, but he accompanies Mary with patience. Bartering allows the high priority activities of your spouse to be enjoyed without separating the couple.

Yet another method is: Taking turns which allows equal reciprocation of interests. John plays handball with his associates every Saturday morning. Then John watches the children while Mary swims at the YMCA in the afternoon.

Another technique to be utilized is creative planning's. Both parties can enjoy themselves without spoiling the fun of the other. Such a situation might be allowing the spouse to dance with someone else at a function, while the sitting spouse continues to converse with friends.

Creative verbal contracts are tailor made by the couple. They are fashioned when both parties possess strong conflicting values or goals.

For example:

Susan wants to return to college full time. Gerry believes that the children should have a full- time mother. Actually Susan agrees, but feels her value of education doesn't necessarily have to conflict with the Traditional value of nurturing.

They settle the dispute by Susan leaving for college after the children get on the school bus and returning before they arrive home. Everyone is satisfied.

IX. TRY TO PUSH YOU OUT OF CONTROL:

This technique teens use to wrest control from the parents.

It is continuing annoying or harassing verbalization (or actions) after the parental's warning to stop. The teen is fully aware that the parent may lose control and begin screaming, crying or exploding in some manner. The teen sits back and smugly thinks how out of control the parent is, and how in control and calm s/he is. This tactic is used by certain males in order to not be deemed the aggressor. When the females become hysterical, they can then be accused of typical female behavior or PMS difficulties.

For Example:

AI : How do you spell dysfunction? Is it spelled D-I-S-F-U-N-C-T-I-0-N?

Martha: No. D-Y-S-F-U-N-C-T-I-0-N.

Al: You're wrong.

Martha looks it up in the dictionary, she points to the word: There see for yourself.

Al: Then the dictionary is wrong.

This type of heckling is clearly meant to wear down the other person's patience. Attempting to reason with a person who has insincere objectives delights them because you have entered their trap of ALICE AND WONDERLAND confusion.

The best method is to call their bluff by refusing to enter or be a part of the plot.

Al burps as he eaten fifteen course holiday meal, and says with a twinkle in his eye, and a knowing glance to other family members that transmits his intentions to pester his wife: That was a nice snack. When are we going to eat?

Martha rises to the bait as she always does: You're still hungry? What do you want? (Martha does not understand that Al is teasing her. She leaves the room sobbing when he continues his tirade.)

Male nonsense undermines the ego-weak woman. Such a woman needs approval. She does not know how to receive it. She must learn to identify the strategy employed and prevent it as in this scene:

Al: The moon is made of cream cheese.

Martha: If that is your belief, then you are welcome to it.

Al: I really believe that.

Martha: I'm on to your tricks. Go torment someone else.

Martha also needs to learn how to reaffirm herself.

X. DECIDE THAT THE RULES DON'T APPLY TO THEM

Definition: Teenagers ignore and deny the rules. Sometimes it's because they deny reality. (Some teens think: other drunks are in auto accidents. It won't

happen to me. I know what I'm doing.)
Teens live in their own world and feel
the rules don't apply to them.

Males frequently establish rules within
the household, but do not feel
compelled to adhere to them.

Some of the other strategies have
previously illustrated this. Here is a
more specific example:

Sam is another husband who only
participates in what he enjoys. He does
not like traveling, dancing, or biking.
Laura does not enjoy his activities of
camping, boating, or walking. However
the majority of the time is spent
camping, boating, or walking. Laura
resolved this problem by suggesting the
following compromise.

Laura: I'm going to Italy with a tour
group.

Sam: When are you going?

Laura: I am purchasing the tickets for
next month for a ten day tour from the
fourth to the fourteenth. The camping

festival is the following week and we can go to that when I return.

Sam: We'll be too tired to go there too.

Laura: Does that mean you are coming with me?

Sam: Of course.

Laura: Great!

Laura took control of her own life and interest. Sam fell in step with her.

Laura can determine her boundaries. Every time that Laura wants to bike, Sam wants to walk. After an unbalanced interval of conforming to his needs, Laura must decide to do her activity, invite her husband to join her, and if he does not, then she can continue her activity separately.

Some more examples:

Susan: I would like some time to rest from the stresses of my job and the kids. Would you watch the kids each Wednesday night while I go to the Health Spa?

Jake: Of Course.

Wednesday night arrives and Susan has on leotards. She grabs her purse as she kisses, Jake and says: "I'll see you later."

Jake: Where are you going?

Susan: Remember you agreed that you would watch the kids so I could go to the Health Spa every Wednesday night?

Jake: You never said a word. I'm going bowling tonight. Jake leaves the house without any further discussion.

Susan might call a baby-sitter, but that will not help Jake's lack of listening skills, nor his refusal to share the same entitlements that he allows himself.

Susan may record the next conversation and replay it for Jake. He probably heard her, but decided that the rules need not apply to both of them, since that's inconvenient for the life style he chooses to live.

Susan might assume his agreement is valid and act on it.

Jake arrives home. Susan greets him with her hat and coat on, and a kiss, and says: Thank you for remembering to watch the kids for me while I go to the health spa. Good bye!

Susan has incorporated several concepts in one statement. She reminds and thanks Jake for his previous agreement instead of looking for a reaffirmation of approval. She rapidly initiates the action, so that there is no time for Bob to object.

Another example:

Bob has disallowed his wife money to spend on household items, clothes for herself or their children, but returns home with a fancy mirrored shadow box with knick- knacks, and a four foot high by three foot in circumference carved, alabaster, column which is beautiful, but lacks any functional purpose. The next day he's angry with his wife because she purchased a pair of shoes that he deemed unnecessary for the infant because the shoes showed no sign of wear. The fact that the child's shoe size went from a size four to a size seven; and that the child was walking on his toes did not convince Bob that the shoes were a necessity. The wife was unable to make Bob understand that toddlers need shoes for support and safety, and that children outgrow shoes every four to six weeks.

This is an extreme example of unilateral rules. One solution that comes to mind is stuffing a bit of cotton in Bob's shoes each day until he becomes aware of the tightness of the shoe. He might develop more empathy.

However with cases such as these, the wife must ask herself: Is it worth the effort?

XI. WORK AT HOODWINKING OTHERS

Definition: The teenager puts a great deal of energy into trying to fool the parents, teachers, or society. An adulterous husband represents himself as a loving spouse to his wife or to society. This camouflage gives the actor a sense of control over his world. The actions are usually discovered and the person is confronted with the misdeed.

Jan was shocked when she discovered her husband's automobile parked outside her friend's house. Jan had taken a different route to the bowling alley. Al was scheduled to be at a Alcohol Anonymous meeting. Jan decided to let Al tell her what happened. She was certain there was a good explanation. When she finished bowling she swung by the same route. Jan was amazed to find herself experiencing deja vu. She shook her head to clear it. Al's car was still there. Al arrived home.

Jan: How was the AA meeting?

Al: Fine.

Jan: Did you get there on time?

Al: Of course, why do you ask?

Jan: Did you stop anywhere on the way?

Al: I'm home the same time I always am, aren't I?

Jan: You watch the time carefully don't you?

Al: I don't want to lose a moment, to be near you.

Jan: Your car was stolen.

Al: No it wasn't. I just got out of it.

Jan: Now you can get back into it and return to Meredith's house where you spent the entire evening.

Al: The AA meetings are held there now.

Jan: And the moon is made of cream cheese. Go spend the rest of your life with Meredith.

Jan requests information, in case there is a reasonable explanation for Al's actions. After assuring herself that he's lying, she cuts to the issue and resolves it.

However she might have egg on her face if the AA meetings are truly held at Meredith's house.

Another case: Peter has been having an affair for one year now. He does not want his co-workers to know because this type of fraternization is frowned on by the corporation. He loves his wife, Karen, and has no intention of leaving her. Lately Margaret, his mistress is pushing for marriage because she's pregnant. The whistle is about to be blown on the entire clandestine affair.

Peter had numerous meetings with the company and with customers at irregular hours, therefore; he had easily carved out a few hours a week at irregular times to visit his madam. To his mistress, he was a romantic knight who would grant her every wish-except that of seeing her on a regular basis To his wife, he was a good provider, a stable lover, and appeared to be the perfect husband. His company found him to be a reliable worker. He presented himself as perfect with each group. Peter is duping himself as much as everyone he deceives. Peter lacks the ability to feel deeply for anyone. Peter is in emotional troubles. He is headed toward sexual addiction. He should seek counseling. However, his male friends envy him. They think he has the best of both worlds. That attitude prevents Peter from questioning his motives.

Margaret gave birth to a boy. She sued Peter for child-support. The blood test proved he was the father, but he was able to convince Karen that he has been wrongly accused. His wife would rather deny his actions, than face the possibility that she can't trust him. A friend of Karen's told her that she had seen Peter, Margaret, and his son together several times. Karen confronted Peter.

What should Karen do? Leave Peter or work with him? Karen decided to stay.

She continues to feel a sense of distrust, and abandonment. She is hostile and resentful, but, she chooses to be loyal. She insists that Peter cease seeing his mistress, but he now wishes to see his son.

Karen must confront the issue that she never really knew the person she married. Peter was not the man he appeared to be. Karen must sort the mirage from reality. Peter is a shell that needs to be filled in. That can only be accomplished by Peter, not by his wife.

Peter's response to the entire situation is a charismatic smile: Can I help it if a little boy is stuck in this body of mine?

Karen: I have to find a man. We can look together and go for counseling or I can look alone and get a divorce. The choice is yours. (Confrontation and refusal to accept the circumstances, unless there is a remedy is the best that Karen and Jan can do.)

As much as I would like this book to answer all questions and help all people, it is not possible to help individuals unless they desire it. I would hope that Peter pursues therapy to fulfill his need for self-affirmation. Peter would be the first to tell you that he is fine because he really believes it. Peter has the world where he wants it, so it is doubtful he will be motivated to tackle his basic limitations that prevent him from the painful maturation process that must be endured to become mature.

Counseling could teach Karen to discard her overwhelming negative feelings. Unpleasant feelings cause the body to become stressed. Stress prevents the immune system from functioning properly, so that Karen will become ill if she chooses to stay and not eliminate her sad ruminations. The negative upsetting thoughts act as if she is ingesting poison daily. I ask my clients if I asked them to take poison on a daily basis-would they do it? The response is a resounding "No".

I point out, "But that is what you are doing on a day by day basis." Karen needs to search for and replace the hurtful situation with fulfilling endeavors in order that she might enrich her sense of self. Then she will happily survive regardless of who is in or out of her life.

XII. COMPETITION

Definition: This is a typical game among youngsters to prove they are bigger, better, stronger, brighter than their peers. Men try to prove similar concepts to their wives.

If a man felt truly superior, he wouldn't have to prove a thing. It would be self-evident. Therefore it is the weak man who has to put his wife down in order that he feels on top.

Denise, in the illustrations below, has found a compliant way to counter Harry's competitive ways.

Harry: Let me do that. You're going to ruin it.

Denise: Be my guest.

On another occasion, Denise was painting the underside of a wooden awning.

Harry joined her: You only do what you want to do. You never do anything difficult.

It's an arduous task, so Denise responds: "Yes you are correct, so I'm finished painting. I wouldn't dream of taking all that pleasure away from you."(She stops painting the house.)

In this example Denise confronts Harry's logic with logic: Harry: I know more than you.

Denise: I would expect that you would know more than me electrically. You have your masters degree in engineering.

Harry: I know more than you in everything.

Denise: Give me a recipe for a Lemon meringue pie.

Harry: "That's not an important thing to know."

Denise: "That's your favorite pie. When you want it next time, you'll have to bake it yourself."

Harry: The store makes it better.

Denise: Then buy it from the store.

In both these scenarios Denise agrees with Harry's assertions. In time Harry will come to realize that his competitive manner is bringing him opposite returns. Competition met assertively will usually correct the problem.

XIII. PLEADING IGNORANCE

Definition: Teens will plead ignorance whenever it suits their purpose. They'll make a nasty crack and then claim they were joking. Pleading ignorance is also used in order to not complete work that is supposed to be done. Youths will state that the teacher never taught them or they don't understand, therefore, they can't do the homework assignment.

Husbands who demoralize their wives,
act as if, they don't know why the wife
is complaining.

Tony: What rag-bin did you get that
dress come from?

Julie: The same one your tie came
from.

Tony: Get your A__ in here and say that
to my face.

Julie: What rag-bin did you get that tie
from?

Tony: What?

Julie: That's right my comment
stemmed from yours.

Tony: Your comment was nasty.

Julie: Think of your comment to me.

Tony: You hurt my feelings.

Julie:: You hurt mine.

Tony: What did I say wrong? I was
telling the truth, but you maligned my
appearance.

Julie: What did you think you did to mine?

Tony: I was right. You were wrong.

Julie: Interesting. Here's a mirror. Look in it.

Tony: (Looking in a mirror) See I told you. I look great!

Tony will continually plead ignorance to(his negative remarks. Like a teen, he refuses to take responsibility for his actions or his words. However Julie might stop Tony dead in his tracks if she replayed the scenario this way:

Tony: What rag-bin did you get that dress from?

Julie: You gave it to me.

Or she might respond: Don't you remember your mother bought it for me last Christmas?

These may be untruths, but delivered with a smile, and a good humored laugh Julie will show there was no intention to deceive, but merely to get his attention long enough to put the put-down in its rightful place. Out!

As for pleading ignorance in order to get out of accomplishing future tasks, Philip thought he had it figured out.

Andrea to Philip: My white top has black specks all over it. Did you wash it with the black jump- pants?

Philip: I was saving water.

Andrea: The top cost $50.00 and the water amounts to a few cents. So how much did you save? t looks like a debit to me.

Danny had stated that he couldn't make a neat bed, but had finally managed to pull the covers up without smoothing the blankets.

Debbie: The covers managed to fly up over the pillow. You'd think that they'd jet themselves into a smooth landing as long as they got that far.

Danny chuckled when he heard the non-threatening recognition of his efforts.

Let us see how Joe and Emma are doing:

Joe agrees to come home early Friday night. He comes in three hours late.

Emma: Remember you promised to get home early tonight.

Joe: I never said that.

He seemed to

Emma: Perhaps my mental tape recorder malfunctioned. I'll make a cassette next time so I can play it back for you.

In all of the above examples, the issue was identified, then a witty response was given. Next a solution must be agreed upon. In most cases, as soon as attention is drawn to the game playing, the intrigue ceases.

The thirteen strategies are used by all age children but are refined by the time one reaches the teen years. Women need to be specific when they deal with children in order that youths will know exactly where, how, and when to fulfill their maturing process. Application of the same principles of maturing can be enlisted with adult subjects as well as youthful ones. Awareness of all the stages of development will certainly help a woman bring up her man.

CHAPTER 8

BRINGING UP HUBBY

(A more intense look at developmental stages. Assuming that the woman is mature and is able to bring up her tad pole children and Frog husband from an adult standpoint.) The Traditional Role is explored in depth.

The first step toward bringing up your husband to become an adult is to have brought up a three year old. If you haven't a child, borrow your neighbors to practice on. The self centered, single minded, possessive narcissistic qualities of the toddler require comparable training that a man needs who is stalled in the toilet training stage.

Baby wants to do everything by himself, but mommy must be on standby and not leave or the infant has a tantrum. Hubby wants his wife to stay home and watch the children (after they have both returned home from outside employment) while he bums around with his buddies (not) recapturing his youth, because he never left it). His rationale is that the wife's role computes to "mother". Of course if you haven't any children, she is a potential mother and since the actual real life product hasn't materialized, he'll gladly oblige by acting out the perfect imitation.

A toddler can wander away from Mom, but screams if Mom goes out of sight. The toddler learns that crying controls Mom. Just as Mommy can't disappear from the infant's sight, wifey can't have a night out with the girls. She might talk to a "male," God forbid. Or even worse than that she might converse with her divorced friends who he believes are instilling all these "freedom" ideas into her head. He does not think his wife can think for herself.

Since hubby is influenced easily by what others think of him, in fact, hurt right to the quick; he is certain that his wife is also not mature enough to listen to another's point of view without aligning herself with it. And should she agree because her problems are similar to those of the dissatisfied friends, he accuses her of being easily swayed. It doesn't occur to him that his behavior determined her choice. Hubby as usual will not take responsibility for any of his actions such as: putting his wife down in front of friends. He's convinced that he's so perfect-his wife shouldn't want to leave him, therefore, it's not necessary to put effort into the relationship. Yet, he has a vague-nagging-feeling that his wife would bound off if he didn't keep a tight rein on her; so he controls as much of her actions as she will allow him to do.

Whenever, wifey gets what he calls "come-uppity" and tries to assert herself he has a repertoire of actions he applies: manipulation, sulking, withdrawing sex or conversation, and/or resources. Some men argue and others use put-downs, and/or obscenities. However, the average marital situation should allow for assertively disagreeing, and creatively using whimsy to deflect conflicts.

Are you still with me? You don't want to leave him? True, what is the chance that you won't get another just like him?

Don't get angry with your mother-in-law for the job she did. Just. make certain that as you bring up hubby you also train your children to be responsible adults.

What if he doesn't beat you, but still is an applicant for childhood-narcissism? What then? If you desperately want a child and don't mind that he is the age-equivalent then be prepared for the most difficult roller-coaster ride of your life. Hang on because the upsets caused by your hubby's immature actions may almost push you off the coaster when it's at it's highest point.

What can you do to revise this situation? You can refuse to be his mommy. Expect abusive language from the Deviant Traditional males such as:

f--- you, c---t, b---h. All have sexual connotations. They are verbal rape.

The adolescent reacts identically. That's encouragement, your husband has aged a bit more than a decade from the one year old level with which he began. However care givers who have survived raising adolescents discover this stage to be one of the most difficult. The youth has an adult mind but lacks experience and empathy.

Frequently we need to raise our own children before we are truly aware of the irritating situations we've cause our parents. But I'm talking about a grown male who is caught in that stage.

If you return anger or obscenities to either the youngster or your husband then you have just sprung the trap that the immature mind has laid for you. (The toddler screams and mommy appears; giving the toddler control over the adult. By the time the toddler is an adolescent the screams are now accusations in order to control Mom,

"All the other parents let their kids go to the Mall. You never let me go. it's a free country, but you imprison me.". The screams have turned into accusations that invite defensive statements.) The obfuscation of issues is as deliberate a reflex action as the toddler's screams. No matter how subconscious the process is, it's just as effective for the adult as for the toddler. (It transposes in masculine language into: That dress is too seductive. Or? any type of attack such as: You didn't make out the checks for the bills.) It gives the attacker the advantage, because it puts the woman on the defense. Now the child/man is in control of the situation.

The Blinded Traditional role (might mitigate some of the man's accusations such as:

Why do you keep such a messy house? (This is often directed toward a woman who is employed outside and inside the home and has children, and no male participation to share the work.)

The male accuses instead of sympathizing: Why are you telling me that your boss hit on you? What are you doing to encourage him? (This may be a projection of his own guilt. He may be having one-night stands.) Why did you stay out till 3:00 a.m. with your friends? (The week before he might have done the same.)

Women personalize the angry attack:

Mrs. D: It must be my fault. I set him off when I asked him to check on the kids. The angry exchanges obfuscate the real underlying issues.

Mr. D: I'm Tired. Why haven't you got dinner ready? Why don't you let me take off my hat before you start f------g with me?

Obscenities could be masking an entire range of unresolved problems. A husband may attack the housekeeping in order to prevent the wife from daring to ask him to share in the work effort.

The male who disallows his mate to report an unwarranted advance from her boss may be concealing his own infidelities. A male who believes his wife may be unfaithful could be professing his own disloyal thoughts or actions. He can only view her by what he thinks he might do in a parallel situation, therefore he concludes she will act as he would.

A spouse that aggressively complains about his wife's commitment very likely is covering up his own lack of marital effort. When he does finally try in the honeymoon stage. It's similar to a child who hasn't done his homework all year and then finally tries to cram all the studying into one night. The male often concentrates all his exertions into a few months in order to compensate her for years of not trying, and then looks for wifely faults to excuse his long list of past mistakes, along with his present slips. The effort becomes too difficult so the honeymoon does not last long.

If the woman is unaware that the marital relationship is shifting towards parent and child inter- reactions, the husband might become her authority figure. This happens when the wife accepts his accusations.

His wife begins to think defensively. "What did I do to cause this?" Reading it now-you may be viewing it in a different perspective, but it is hard not to blame yourself. Your subconscious reasoning often becomes, if it is my fault, then I can control and improve the situation.

In my practice I find this to often be the way that women react. Therefore, women act nicer, are more tolerant, nurturing and kind hoping that the mate will respond in kind.

However this type of mate instead, returns additional insensitive reactions and behaviors. Often causing his wife to re-evaluate her situation. Others may still feel responsible for his actions, then, the lack of improvement creates a downward spiral of decreased self-confidence. She becomes the co-conspirator, accepting all the responsibility for the couple's dysfunction, therefore, allowing the man-child to remain at his present level. Hopefully, most women will recognize the male's ploy to ensnare them in a guilt-trap, and will disavow the husband's false accusations.

Yet, many women allow themselves to be controlled by men. Men control in much the same way as a toddler. The toddler feels out of control and his sense of security depends on his ability to control his mother's responses for his needs. Women in turn, nurture men without demanding co-operation thus nourishing the inappropriate responses, instead of fostering adult to adult reactions. It is truly a conspiracy that must be recognized and exterminated.

Mrs. Co-conspirator needs to ask herself, 'Whose problem is this? Mine or his?' Mrs. Co. will probably consider it her problem, so that question won't help her. Why not create a different script. Why not think about your situation as if it belongs to a friend. She is relating her situation. What would you say to her? Is your answer different this time? Or perhaps it might help if you observe children. If your spouse's mannerisms compliment those of the youths you're observing, then challenge yourself to developing communication skills and techniques which would work for any age person.

Now, consider the Behavioral Modification Conditioning which alters actions that would be applicable and similar to the limited inter-communication skills between man and animal. This technique reminds me of my female cat that after seven years of cohabitation decided that: at bedtime, she wanted to be put outside, then be allowed back in an hour later, and continued this alternating arrangement until the wee hours of daylight. Putting the cat to sleep permanently entered my mind but that would be my last option. In order to wake me, the cat had scratched my face, meowed in my ear, and walked up the length of my sleeping form. I had responded with a push, a slap, and yelling; none of which was successful. I decided to ignore all her antics. For one week she walked the length of me, screeched in my ear, and tugged at me. I made believe I was sleeping. For the remaining ten years of her life she never pestered me since that week when I ignored her.

That conditioning reaction is as effective with humans. As a child I was conditioned by silence after becoming accustomed to my mother's continuous raucous nagging. She really got my attention when for two whole days she refused to talk to me! I wondered what I had done that was so horrendous as to deserve silence. Silence can be the deafening roar that gets another's attention.

However, if you never say anything, ever, don't expect that this method will work for you. It is the change in technique that is effective. Work on improving your communication skills.

This example will illustrate communication skills:

Mr. Controller: Are there any men attending your meeting? (When the response is negative): Are you sure? I don't want you driving the car. You might get mugged. You don't have any good friends if they are not willing to pick you up and take you to the meeting."

What's Mr. Controller really relating to you? He's fearful that he is not attractive enough to keep you from wandering. He believes that if he can prevent you from using the car, you'll be unable to meet anyone before or after the meeting. Therefore the put-down message that you have no friends is instead an anxious message to maintain control over your freedom. Let's assume that he has no concrete basis for his concern, but you personalize the negative messages that you are not worthy of friendship because you have accepted his redefinition of your relationships. Then you also assent to his opinion that you are incapable of making friends.

The nursery rhyme: sticks and stones will break my bones but names will never hurt me, is inaccurate. Both sexes are defenseless against knives, and guns, but if you accept his definition of your attributes then your sense of self-worth is damaged. Internalizing his dictates, now secures you as his prisoner.

Instead of integrating the message; analyze its significance as I did in the previous paragraph. Now you are prepared to communicate effectively with him.

Here is a situation to illustrate how to deal humorously with a controlling male:

Mr. Controller: Who is at the meeting with you? Are there males there?

Wife: I'll request a list of the club membership from the secretary tonight.

Mr. C: You'll make me look like a fool.

Wife: You said it. I didn't.

Or You might note that you are aware he feels threatened whenever you are not in his presence. You will have to elaborate on this further with sincere specific information on what qualities you consider to be his forte. For example, if you admire his good provider qualities and find him an excellent sexual partner, then state this and as much more about him that you are pleased with. Remind him that you love him and show him your affection openly. If you are dealing with a classic narcissistic, this approach will be effective only after multiple years, if then. However if your husband has been conditioned by society to believe that entitlement is his right based on the Traditional Roles which promote machismo reactions, then the reassurance will relieve the anxiety, because you are understanding his position so compassionately that he will feel comfortable with letting you leave his side.

For example the couple might converse thus:

Mrs. Controller: Thank you for loving me so much that you want to protect me constantly. But who will be your guardian angel tonight? I'll attend all your meetings with you-to protect- you. After all two people can provide a better defense than one.

Mr. Controller: That's not practical I can take care of myself.

Mrs. C: Touché! Listen to yourself. It's my response to you.

The Traditional role obligates a man to protect his wife. The Traditional role has been subliminally ingrained into both genders of our culture so that we are unaware of its domination. Consider this: Which would you rather have first? A male or a female child. If you answer

was a male, think about your reasons.
Can you find a logical reason or only a
strong feeling of why that is your
preference? Unwritten and non-
verbalized rights have a stronger
bastion than those we can identify.

The Traditional role places the male as
the keeper of economic resources, the
final authority over domestic issues and
major decisions, the arbitrator for the
amount and time sex takes place, the
protector, and imposer of gender
separate activities. This role was
originally brought over from England,
Ireland, Italy, etc. as part of out
ancestors' cultural heritage.

The Traditional role is slowly gasping its
last breath, but it's not extinguished.
The Traditional roles entitle men to
special rights and privileges. Some men
cling to and extend these rights to
determine when-where-and-what
resources of time, and money that the
wife may use for her benefit. The
percentage of the female population,
who is not employed outside the home

and who has the responsibility of full-time housewife and mother, finds herself in a fancy prison without bars. This demography of housewives who are full-time mothers have no one to converse with, and little to converse about because small children capture their undivided attention during waking hours. Discussing housecleaning is good for one night for the rest of one's entire life. So what has she to discuss for the next thirty-thousand, six hundred and fifty nights of her life? (In case you're wondering how I obtained that figure. Compute ten years of a child's life times 365 days in each year. After ten years she will probably return to the work force and by that time have a more interesting conversational input.) Of course she appears boring!

Prisoners must obtain permission to make calls, must make them at specific times, have limited financial resources, plus they are restricted to one area. Compare the Traditional housewife to our convicts. What pray-tell, is the difference in life styles? Perhaps the only difference is that women think they have chosen their prison, while the criminal must take whatever accommodations he has been given.

Women cling to the female Traditional Roles of softness, compassion, nurturing, gentleness, passiveness, and non obtrusiveness to dictate their femininity which retains them as a compliment to the male macho role.

Women say: When my husband ignores me, I can't get on the telephone with my friends. Even though the man hushes her attempts at conversation with him so that he can watch TV. Some woman consent to his dictatorship: They say: He won't let me drive at night. He won't let me use the car. He won't give me money.

I see many women making no choices to redirect their environment. Instead women clients tell me they have no freedom because they see no options available to them. The Traditional Roles indenture the wife when an observer, either peer, friend, or in-law remark; she isn't performing her wifely obligations when she does not adhere to the male-prescribed-roles. Her preference as the major child-rearer chain her to the house. In other situations the husband points out that working outside the home would only pay for the baby sitter. There is no economic gain. However, more importantly the subliminal Traditional traits regulate the internal world of these women.

Traditional roles obligate women to nurture. Even those women freed from these roles, usually continue to conform with the child-care obligations. Males reinforce the Traditional Role by demands and often reiterate the boundaries beyond the original concepts. The original Traditional role equally divided the work responsibilities. The men accomplished the muscular labour and the women took care of a household multiplied by children. Presently the majority of women have outside employment, household chores, and raising children. All the roles have been restructured to fit the needs of a different society. Moreover, the remodeling is often done without forethought, but the owner's perception of the original concepts gives the female a guilt complex because she is incorporating both the Traditional Role and the Equal Role concepts into a single unit. Even if the husband proclaims her freedom to "go out with the girls," the wife often has an invisible restraint (the Traditional constraints) that restricts her from allowing herself equality.

As a counselor I observe that in a number of cases the wife underestimates her mates love for her. The wife could simply state, "I'm taking the car tonight". "I made out a check today for new curtains." "I am calling my friend, but I will-put the phone down as soon as you are ready to talk with me." As soon as these women act in an (adult) egalitarian status, most men will meet them at that stance.

Just as water finds its own level; women who quietly but determinedly sustain equilibrium, discover that they maintain it. Currently in our society, both are acting more maturely as women are employed outside the home.

Yet the Traditional Role ubiquitously remains when:

1. Women are the primary housekeepers and nurturers after-work-hours.

2. Women are still not on the same salary level as men for the same work week even though they have similar educational degrees. Employers often change the same duties title to fit the gender who is performing it. (A secretary in a firm may be performing her boss's obligations, but her title restricts the pay.)

3. Women frequently live at the husband's selection of residential-area without a mutual decision making process.

4. Women unthinkingly and constantly bow to the husband's choice of recreation, and socialization. (For example: Jack offers a selection of five restaurants at which to have dinner. Jill suggests a different selection. Jack reviews his original selection ignoring Jill's input. This happens over-a period of many years. It is a typical case.

Jill complains and Jack responds that he always gives her a vote. Jill states: I have as much freedom as the Russian citizens. They are given a right to decide what the administrators have already decided upon.

5. Women characteristically clean up after a dinner at friends homes as the men retire to the TV room. (When I commented on this to my oldest son recently, he stated that women don't want him in the kitchen. He gets in their

way. I suggested he try. He did and no one told him to get lost!)

6. Women step-aside when the man disciplines the child. (There are major exceptions to this in step-parenting situations.)

If any of the above one through six options are your life situations, then you're not on an equal stance with your husband.

Equal roles are shared communications and decisions. Frequently the male gives the appearance of mutual agreements but then assumes that his vote holds more weight. It's as if the largest person (the one with the most constituents?) has more influence.

The struggle for equality is not a dead issue. It is fought on the home lines in lonely unrecognized battles. Equality and narcissistic attitudes don't room well together. Narcissus by definition shines its spot light upon the one alone who must star continually.

Most men are not narcissistic by nature. They have been unknowingly primed for the role. By the time our sons reach maturity, and women have realized the confusion of cultural dictates it's too late for parental revision of the cultural-concepts for that generation. Now, it falls in the wife's domain to lead a one woman revolution. Often, her husband sees no need for alterations. He's content as he is. The only hope is to educate husbands now before the children are born. Then the new generations of both genders will have a chance to be equal.

Now here is the paradoxical shaker. Women cannot train their husbands to do anything.

Women cannot control anyone but, themselves. No one can be controlled unless they chose to be controlled. (Exceptions such as brute force or brainwashing will not be entertained as an option within the context of this book. Although these situations exist in society, this book will deal with only the varying degrees of minor deviances from the behavioral norm). The greatest paradox is that as long as no one controls another person's behavior, the non-controller has the greatest degree of control over, not only the person who she is not trying to control, but also over life.

How does this happen? A non-controlling person does not require a husband to behave in any specific way. However, the compliant wife may request that certain behaviors upset her in varying ways that she describes Most women do this. However, in order to be the most effective she must outline the effect the situation is having upon her in a clam, quiet manner. Women will come to my office and say: I am going to divorce him. Then return home and never mention the extreme feelings. She should not be threatening, but merely factually state the effect upon the marriage. She must have tight control over her own emotions and actions. She must be willing to accept the consequences of her words and follow through on them. (Go for counseling alone. Go for a separation or divorce, if necessary, but don't deliver an effect without being willing to act on your words. Otherwise you lose all credibility. The next time your comments are taken as a threat.)

For example:

The wife states that her husband's smoking is creating a pre-cancerous condition in her lungs from breathing stale smoke, therefore, she must have a smoke-free room.

She uses the first person pronoun, giving an "I" message:

Wife: If you choose to smoke please do so elsewhere. I can't breathe when you smoke in the same room. My eyes smart. I feel sick to my stomach. My head feels as if someone is tightening a vice on it.

Then acknowledge that he doesn't have to stop smoking, only stop in your presence.

If the husband disregards this message, the wife must outline an increase in the level of future danger; That his behavior is affecting her ability to live, illness-free and that she will find another residence immediately. Then if her husband again disregards her factual report of her needs, she must move out, for her own chances of survival (I use a life/death circumstance in order to make the point dramatically clear.).

She might say: I love you but, I am not going to die for you. Unless you smoke elsewhere I will have to leave you.

Lesser problems may be addressed in the same manner. State the behavior that you wish to change, state the facts and emotions which correspond with the behavior in the first person only, and the consequences of the current action. Then be willing to act on the consequences if action if necessary. Sometimes the consequences are beyond your control and are in the hands of God. However, we can usually give God a hand by acting in our own interests.

Try showing him either by acting out a scene or drawing one. You might act in a clowning manner. Or draw yourself with bulging eyes and green face with smoke swirls hovering over your sunken skull. Anything to make the point.

In whatever manner the non controller wishes to portray her comic reaction, she is now directing her own actions. When the husband perceives that her resolve is mature and persistent, he usually changes his actions. The husband has two alternatives: cease smoking in the home and other areas when his wife is present or- stop smoking entirely. The choice is his and either way he complies with his wife's statement that clearly identifies the problem, her feelings, and the solution.

If he decides to smoke in her presence and she leaves him, he must live with the consequences of his own choice; but realize that at no time was he manipulated. The likelihood is that he will remain, and pick one of the first two options available to him.

Therefore the contradiction is that in not attempting to govern anyone, but yourself, creates control and harmony to your life and surroundings. This is the epitome of equality.

Here is an example of the above premise.

Sarita wants Sidney to spend time with her. She usually berates him, for the long hours that he works, as soon as, he walks in the door. Lately Sidney is putting in longer and longer hours. Sarita is primarily feeling rejected because Sidney no longer shows the romantic interest that she craves. Sarita assesses her own behavior and recognizes that her past attacks would not warm anyone's heart. She puts into action what she really feels. Sarita decides to greet him daily with her sexiest apparel, "Hi handsome I've missed you a lot today! I'm anticipating this weekend. Let's plan something special to do." Sidney's initial response is surprise and then delight that he's welcomed home. Next, he refuses all overtime. He eagerly returns home every evening now.

Finding that disgruntled behaviors creates marital distance, Sarah exchanges them for optimistic pleasant expressions of her desires. Sidney complied with her wishes because they were his aspirations also.

Unfortunately some women have forgotten that love is their wish. They have become so resentful that they can't bring themselves to attempt a reversal of the situation. Women turn off sexually when there is an altercation. Men behave in the opposite manner. They believe that lovemaking will show their willingness to make up and forget the incident. The women becomes enraged because she doesn't phantom the man's intentions. Neither gender feels understood.

One survey determined that the happiness quota of Traditional and Partnership Roles after fifty years. The Partnership couples were one hundred percent happy, but, only thirty-five percent of the Traditional couples only claimed contentment. The half-century Partnership-marriages discovered equal caring, sharing, respect, and love, who mutually followed the same guidelines. What was good for one was good for the other. It would be safe to say that people that think together, are loyal together, then live happily together. (Ever after-if you wish, but it is a process that involves daily effort to maintain the fairy tale.)

Egalitarian Roles establishes a new kingdom of royalty, where every husband is the prince and his wife is the princess.

If you want to skip ahead to physical abuse, go to Chapter 20. Deviant juvenile regressed men are not past shoving, blocking her exit, punching, slapping or simply holding her down. In physical abuse cases her options are: fight back and get badly beaten, back down, go for counseling to determine other options, or secretly leave after he has left for work.)

CHAPTER 9

FOR THE RUSHED Business/Housewife/

Mother WOMAN

(A menagerie of animals: Dogs, Cats, FROGS? Any animal to make the point.)

Business women have little time for fairy tales so I'll come straight to the point. Gender differences are physically determined as proven by electric monitoring of the brain. However I do use real incidents to create emotional Ah Ha connections. Therefore my observations of specie differences of cats and dogs has a metaphoric connection to gender difference. Dogs will represent the male gender and cats the female.

I had a dog who chased, then sat on our cat before she could reach the safety of the tree. As she squealed with ears low, he would look innocently around in an upwards circular motion as if to say, "I'm not sitting on the cat. Do you see a cat? I'm just resting." When he tired of the game, he'd walk away without a backward glance. In time, our cat merely squatted until the dog relinquished his position. Years later, (with a different set of animals) my two independent cats played hide and seek with our dog. The dog would squeal and lick his nose after he caught up with either of the cats. One day I entered the game only to find that, when found, the cat took her claw and dug it into my hand like a half moon. It hurt for months.

The play perspectives are tolerated between domestically reared pets in the same household but, are hardly appreciated by the one on the receiving end. Gender differences whether culturally imposed or physically inherent cause just as much discord among humans. Men want to make love after a angry tirade to show that they hold no grudge and all is forgiven. Women take that as being akin to rape. Women want to resolve differences first, develop a romantic ambience and then make love.

It proves to women's self-fulfilling prophesy that men do not listen. Very few men even understand the emotional concept the wife is discussing, so the rift becomes larger.

To make matters worse some women are intimidated by men. Not you? Have you ever dented a fender, but blamed it on a shopping cart rolling into it? Have you ever said that a friend gave you last years dress because you didn't want to face the inquisition of "We can't afford that right now." Have you ever turned him down because you were turned off by his actions, but said instead, "I have a headache."? Have you ever had a male friend from a chat room as a friend, but kept the innocent conversation secret because of his jealous rages? Have you ever said you have to work so you could lunch with your girlfriends? If any of these examples or similar ones like it are part of your reactions; then you are either intimidated, not getting through to your alpha male, or having problems allowing yourself assertive rights.

The stages of development in chapters five and six are meant to free women of whatever intimidation they might retain by comedically creating a nonthreatening image. A nurse was unable to respond to a physician even when she spoke to him on the telephone. I suggested she visualize him naked the next time they spoke. She reported that it worked. In fact she had difficulty restraining her laughter.

Utilize whatever solution works for you. Moreover, if you are following the dictate that women must be nice and nurturing or they are not ladies, perceiving your mate in another manner might help you to be firm and caring but persevering your objective.

Do you feel it is not a women's place to be blunt? Is he supposed to read your mind? How will you know if he really wants to please you if you don't make your needs clear? (Electrically monitoring the brain illustrates that when puzzled, men react with 100% of the left (logistics) hemisphere. (That's why the bottom line suits men better). Women react with both hemispheres. Women's right hemisphere react about 33% as emotionally/creatively and about 98% on the logical left side. These brain differences create vast differences in perceptions between a man and a woman.

Are you usually clear, but there is a delicate subject difficult to discuss: Sex? In-laws? Money? Give him a multiple choice question, Presenting all the options for whatever it is and then ask him to select the one that best fit his notions.

Have you ever been annoyed when your husband cleaned, cooked, shopped or did any type of domestic duty? Do you realize that you're following the traditional duties now, not your husband?

Unilateral decisions of the male to: purchase large items such as computers, cars, fishing equipment, golf clubs, or any other toys; determine that the female do a larger portion of the workload whether it is child care, housework, or bookkeeping; decide on the time or amount of sexual relations. If you accept his perceptions carte blanche then the traditional role is having its way again. This category creates such resentment that often the female's thought crystalizes into, "I do everything myself. What do I need a man for?" The man's sense of entitlement to select whatever decision or duty suits him is a derivative of the societal traditional messages which are rapidly being revolted against by today's women.

Some women fall for the flattering line, "You can do it better than I." That may be so, but in many cases it is just another form of manipulation so that the male might watch TV, play with the computer, or maintain his hobbies or friendships that keep him from servicing the families needs. Regardless of whether the wife is a computer widow or a golf widow; These men remain inaccessible for friendly conversation. In the same manner as the adolescent who will divert your attention to what he wants to do rather than what you want him to accomplish.

Lastly the clinging male that won't allow you to go anywhere without him may be just what you want. If that is your romantic desire, and it is fulfilling, then enjoy it. If however, you feel it is another way to control your time, then view it as stage of development and treat it accordingly with laughter.

The next Chapter 10, gives examples of how to further the males' developmental growth. The wife, Tak, starts the process of making her husband Mal a prince. Tak illustrates how to deflect conflicts with her own brand of hilarity. These stories demonstrate new approaches to ponder.

CHAPTER 10
GROWING WEEDS OR VEGETABLES?

Frogs or humans? Weeds or Vegetables? What is happening in this scenario?

Examples: A titillative reframing of a family situation follows:

Mal, a two hundred and fifty pound, six-foot muscular husband had slipped off his shoes. When he went to arise, he said to his wife Tak, "Put my shoes on."

Tak, a petite five-foot-one, blond, looked elaborately around. She checked under pillows. She investigated the areas behind the doors. She brought in the kitchen ladder, climbed it, and looked over the crevices between the screws which held it on. Her husband, Mal said, "What are you doing?" Tak said, "I thought I heard a child asking me to put his shoes on, but perhaps it is a Pixie that I can't see."

Mal responded, "What are you talking about? There are no kids here, just you and me. Have you gone crazy?"

Tak intensified her search. She peered out the window, and scrutinized the under the windowsill. "The elves must be here somewhere, I heard one say, "Put on my shoes'".

Mal is vexed. "That was me telling you to put on my shoes."

Tak laughed. "That couldn't be you. A grown man would never ask anyone to dress him."

Mal sheepishly began to put his feet into his shoes.

It was time for dinner, Tak was busy preparing the meal, she asked Mal to help by getting the baking dish out since her hands were messy from the meat loaf she was mixing. Mal ignored her request. Good naturedly, Tak explained what she was doing, and why she'd appreciate his help. Mal walked out of the room.

Tak washed her hands and went into the living room and turned on the TV. After two hours, Mal wondered aloud when the meal was going to be ready. Tak turned a surprised face towards Mal, "Why we're going out to eat. I'm too tired to fix a meal after working all day."

Mal's face had tornado signals written all over it. His loud dissonance would have blown down the nearest tree. "You're a woman. You're supposed to cook. I'm too tired to go out. Now get into the kitchen and make my meal!"

Newly wedded Tak arouse, but headed for the door. Mal blocked her exit. Tak gave Mal a big kiss. She rolled her eyes enticingly. "There's breakfast in bed or dinner at the diner. Which one do you prefer right now?" Malls anger dissipated into a chuckle, then a peel of laughter. "You won't get away with this," he said as he placed his arm in hers and walked with her to the car.

On the way to the diner, Mal mused openly, "You wouldn't put my shoes on, but you expected me to help you with dinner."

Tak said, "Yesterday I was at Susan's house. Her three year old daughter demanded that Susan put her shoes on. Julia had a fit. Susan sent her to her room. I looked at you and all I saw was Julia's tantrum. You can't be serious. I work as many hours as you do. I expect your help."

Mal defended his position. "I carry heavy boards all day. I hammer and my arms are tired."

"I'm worried about you. Perhaps we should make an appointment with the doctor. Maybe you've a heart problem that no one ever picked up."

"I'm as strong as an ox."

"That's not what I'm hearing. You're too exhausted to put on your own shoes or work with me in the kitchen. I'm very concerned about you."

Mal hung his head. When he looked up, his eyes twinkled, "I can't put a thing over on you."

You can put yourself over me anytime."

They both smiled at each other. Mal moved over in the booth and put his arm proudly around Tak's shoulder, "I'll dress myself, but I'll never be caught dead in the kitchen."

"I'll speak to the Maitre de when we leave, perhaps we can make permanent reservations for two at 6:30 p.m. each evening.". Tak's impish grin persisted.

After a pleasant romp in bed and refreshing sleep the two awakened. Mal said, "My toe nails need cutting. It's hard to reach down. Will you do them?"

"I'll do yours and you'll do mine. Deal?"

"Deal"

Marriage is complicated by children, but extracting amusement from their otherwise irritating battles gives the couple a reflection of themselves, that they might objectify and then apply the same capriciousness with themselves.

Since then, Tak and Mal's family has expanded to include the young children named Matt, Sean, and Terry. The children are five, four, and two respectively. A picnic is planned. Tak prepares the eggs for salad. She cuts the onions and celery. She peels the potatoes, boils them and adds the mayonnaise and other ingredients. She climbs into the difficult to get at spaces for the seldom used Tupperware, plastic utensils, napkins, cups and basket. Mal is watching a TV sports review. Tak bathes and dresses all three children, and herself. Tak drags the chairs, folding table, and vacuum bottles up from the basement. She fills the vacuums with coffee and lemonade. Mal says, "What's taking you so long? Let's go!" After four hours of effort she has everything accomplished. Tak says, "I'm ready. Let's go."

"Let's go?!" Mal says, "I haven't shaved yet. It'll only take me twenty minutes."

Tak silently decides that she will scotch tape a picture of a clean shaven man's face on the TV the next time they are preparing an outing. Tak knows the value of patience. Speaking now would ruin the picnic they had planned.

The thing that Mal expects and gets, is Tak's co-operation loading the car with the food, hardware, children's car seats and of course, the children.

Mal and Tak are proud parents. They enjoy watching the children romp and run with each other. Tak's gentleness is reflected in Matt's protective ways with his chubby blond two-year-old sister, Terry. Sean is comical but mimics Matt. Sean insists that he wants the grass that is between Matt's legs. Five year-old Matt, moves to accommodate Sean reseating himself with his legs out sketched. Four-year-old Sean, again decides that the lawn between Matt's fleshy legs is greener than anywhere else in the park. Matt pulls the grass out and gives it to Sean. Sean screams, "I wanted to do it myself. He always gets the best spot. He always can do anything he wants." Matt pulls at the waist line of his shorts, shrugs as he moves backwards, not knowing how to please Sean.

Tak had read in the park pamphlet, that there are thirty-six miles of grassy park, but the lean Sean is unhappy unless he has the green by Matt's legs. The mirthful irony escapes Sean. Tak diverts Sean's attention, "Let's go for a walk Sean, and see if we can find a fox." Sean sends a smug look towards Matt. Sean takes his mother's hand, "What color will the fox be?"

"We'll find that out when we locate one." A few hours later, Sean and Mom return. Sean excitedly tells his story to his siblings. "I asked Mom when were we going to see a fox? We were just standing there, and a fox came right up to my hand!"

Mom said, "You would have thought it was a stage and someone pushed the fox on stage, right on cue!" Mom's joy diminished as she noticed that Mal seemed itchy to leave.

(Living in the moment increases family and marital happiness. It is the absorption of the little things such as in the previous and next paragraph.)

The children scampered around. Tak and Mal quietly packed and moved the things into the car.

At home both parents moved the items into the kitchen. Mal turned on the TV while Tak put away the leftovers, prepared the kids for bed and then joined Mal in the living room.

Mal stated that he would like a cup of coffee. Tak said, "T¬hat would be nice. Get one for me, too."

Mal said, "I want you to get one for me."

"Did you break your legs and arms today? I hadn't noticed," Tak bantered. "I'm tired. It's the first time I've sat all day. Please get me a cup when you make yours."

Mal complied. After finishing his coffee, he turned off the TV in the middle of the program. "I'm going to bed now." Mal gave Tak a meaningful look that demanded she accompany him. Tak responded to the stare. "Because it's your bedtime, it's supposed to be mine?" She makes light of the understood restrictions. "Il need to wind down after the day's activities. And I want to see the rest of this show. Then I'll join you."

"How can we make love if you're not in bed?"

"I don't remember suggesting any such thing!" She paused to allow Mal to consider that. "Lovemaking goes on all day, by the way that you respect me and my needs and wants, by the co-operative efforts you make in my behalf. When did that happen?"

"I don't know what you're talking about. I got you coffee." Mal sulked as he left for the bedroom.

The next day Tak constantly shifted the picnic-cellar items that Mal had left for her to put away. She cleaned the house, and baked a birthday cake. As the day wore on she became angrily determined to leave the equipment for Mal to return to the basement. According to her tally, she had done the major work of the picnic, and the so-called heavy male's job was also left for her to accomplish.

As Tak watched Mal walk up the driveway a plan took place in her head. She put the chairs in front of the door, just as the items had cluttered access to the kitchen cupboards, she decided that they looked right in front of the door.

Tak attempted to open the door, but the folding chairs blocked his entrance. He swore and pushed. Finally he asked Tak to remove them. Tak widened her eyes, "Oh were they in your way? They've been in my way all day. " Tak smiled.

Mal understood Tak's irritation. He put the things away.

Tak's humorous restructuring of her situation, a neutral tone, assertiveness, and empowering herself based on her insights that the male labels woman as a synonym for slave; helped her to resolve the situation without friction . Tak's only concern is that Sean will emulate Mal's behavior before she can stem all the aspects of gender injustice.

Note Tak and Mal's family structure. It will live on, as a pattern of family style and discipline, into the next generation for the children: Terry, Sean, and Matt. Mal's participation or lack of it will set the model. Sean is already emulating the sulking actions of his father, Mal.

Tak's fear is based in the reality of Traditional dictates left over from all the ethnic immigration groups which settled this country which continue to create discord from one generation to another. The bible's dictates of male-exclusive-authority causes American couples to lose interest in one another sexually, which anthropologically speaking is an excellent form of contraception. Think about it. If one does not give or get respect as an adult from ones spouse, they hardly wish to celebrate with intercourse. Therefore, a non-respected female becomes as celibate as she can manage with excuses such as: "I have a headache. I'm awfully tired." Celibacy is the best form of birth control. However, we have contraceptives now. We don't need discord to keep couples from enjoying each other.

Unfortunately discord is prevalent in a large segment of the population, in which yesterday's and today's child-rearing practices creates the pattern for future generational behavior.

The next Chapter, Grow Up, suggests how attitudes established during childhood, shape adulthood.

This story, plus others that you will read in succeeding chapters of this book, hit vital nerves in women and hopefully will become the healing voices of direction for both genders.'

CHAPTER 11

GROW UP

Some more froggy caricatures:

Andrew wanted a toy truck for Christmas. He drove his parents wild with his continual requests. He played with it all Christmas Day and then never looked at it again.

Andrew wanted to marry Betsy so badly that he swept her off her feet. He played with her on the wedding night and, then one year later ignored her .

Betsy tried to tantalize Andrew. She did a bump and grind to burlesque music blaring loudly as she was setting the dining room table. Andrew asked as he perused the newspaper without looking up, "When is dinner going to be ready?"

Betsy donned a tea apron, and served a sumptuous meal she had prepared. She slithered next to him. Betsy put the tray of desserts on the floor and passed them between her legs up to his place on the table. She stripped off one piece of clothes at a time. Dangling her bra in front of the newspaper, Betsy then sensuously dripped honey from her nude breasts. Andrew waved the bra away as if it were an offending fly. The music undulated as she fanned several napkins over her body erotically flinging them at intervals towards different corners of the room.

Then Andrew rose, stretched, and excitedly said, "Honey, Let's go to bed. And watch the baseball playoffs. I don't want to miss it! How did these napkins get all over the floor? You really shouldn't be so careless." Betsy stalked off. Andrew called from the bedroom, "Where are you?"

Betsy angrily entered, went to Andrew's bureau and got out his long red insulated hunting underwear and with exaggerated efforts put them on. Then she went to her bureau and put on her jogging clothes. Next she arrayed herself in Andrew's hunting pants and jacket. She slipped on his boots and then climbed in beside him, pulling the covers over her. Andrew barely glanced at her. "Cold?", he said. Andrew quickly became engrossed in the plays, "Holy cow! Look at that!" His hand groped for her arm. He shook it excitedly. "Wow!," he said, as he was still looking intensely at the TV. Betsy leaped from the bed, undressed and put on a sexless nightie. The game ended as she climbed back into bed.

Andrew pulled Betsy's stiff body towards him, climbed aboard her and gave two jerks, rolled over and went to sleep. The end of a perfect evening!

The next morning Betsy packed her bags and left. Andrew returned home, sat down to read the paper, awaiting his dinner. As darkness set in, he began to look around for Betsy. He became certain that there was foul play. Betsy could only be gone if someone had kidnapped her. He was amazed to find a note in her handwriting pinned on the empty hangers in her clothes closet.

Dear Clueless,

When you regain your sight and hearing, don't contact me. I'll contact you.

Betsy

Andrew telephoned every friend, relative, and acquaintance that he and Betsy knew but, no one knew where his wife was. Andrew told Betsy's mother, "How could she do this to me? I provide a nice home for her. I work hard. She'd better be back by tomorrow night or I'm through with her!" Andrew told Betsy's friends, "I'm the best catch of the day. How could she leave me? You know she never wore an apron when she cooked? She's not the best homemaker, you know but, I put up with her." To his acquaintances he said, "I'm a red hot lover. She'll never find another like me."

As the days rolled by Andrew found constant fault with Betsy, "She was a cold fish-frigid." He told his business friend, "Why the last time we screwed, she held her self stiff as a board" He told her parents, "She took forever to serve the food, and it tasted like paste. She should be grateful that I bore with her novice ways. Let her know that I'll forgive her if she comes home by tonight."

Betsy sent him a copy of HOW TO TRAIN YOUR HUSBAND TO BECOME AN ADULT. He read it and began to weep, "That's me. That's me. What have I done?" Andrew spread the word that he would change. Betsy called. Andrew apologized. Betsy returned.

The first night home Betsy was watching TV when Andrew arrived home from work. Betsy's feet were crossed on the cocktail table, a half-finished piece of pizza was beside her. "What's for dinner?" Andrew said.

Betsy was engrossed with her soap opera. Andrew went to the kitchen and found a pizza box and pulled a piece out to munch on. He sprawled down beside Betsy and began to nibble her ear. Then he stroked her breast and told her he loved her. Betsy appeared not to notice. The soap finished. She turned off the TV., "Let's go to bed. There's a good horror movie on." In the bedroom, Betsy snapped on the TV set, "Ooooh isn't that gruesome?," she said without glancing at Andrew.

Andrew got up, put on his long underwear, clothes and boots and climbed into bed. Betsy glanced at him as he climbed into bed with his boots on. She burst out laughing. Andrew said, "I read HOW TO TRAIN YOUR HUSBAND TO BECOME AN ADULT. I know you are reversing the scene. How long will this last?" He joined the comic relief of laughter. Betsy said, "Until I feel the release of revenge and we become equal."

Andrew came home the second night and headed for the kitchen. Betsy was watching another soap opera but, she noted his actions. Andrew scrapped some carrots and cooked some hamburgers. (The only menu he had ever learned.)

Andrew lit some candles and put out the lights as he said, "Dinner is served." He put on a cassette containing soft romantic music. "How was your day?" he asked Betsy. "The boss gave me a hard time."

"What happened?" Andrew asked with sincere concern. Betsy explained that the boss tried to hit on her.

Andrew said, "Why didn't you ever tell me this before?"

Betsy said, "When have I ever gotten your ear?"

"The ball is in your court. That's five-love, your serve dear."

"Why don't we make the score, Love-Love? We don't need competition. We need equality."

"That's ten-love. Oh I'm sorry. It'll take me time to learn the new criteria. Will you bear with me?" Andrew said.

"New standards appeal to me. I'll wait as long as we agree on the guidelines. I get home from work an hour before you do. I'll probably have completed dinner by then."

"O.K. I'll serve the meal and clean up afterwards. I'll even put the dishes into the dishwasher."

"Don't strain your pitching arm Dear."

That was a cheap shot."

"I know. I couldn't resist it. It'll take time for me to readjust to this situation too."

The third night Betsy served a delicious meal. Andrew complimented her on its excellence.

Andrew cleared the table. Betsy entered the kitchen one hour later. The dirty dishes were still sitting on the counter. Betsy returned to the living room and smiled sweetly, "The dishes

await my lord and master."

I'll let you finish the story but, only if you end it with Betsy and Andrew comparing their days, discussing their differences, respecting each other egos, and sharing the mutual work.

Comedic approaches will often gain the much needed attention, however, as you observe in this story Betsy was unable to obtain it, at first. She needed a one on one eye contact which included her husband's sense of awareness in order for her to be successful. Moreover, Betsy needed to obtain a consensus of opinion instead of her unilateral goal of lovemaking. A direct request of, "Would you like to make love this evening?" would suffice. Otherwise one sided goals remain self centered which results in dissatisfaction.

What's more, if a direct request is continually disregarded, then one must establish clear concise messages that convey the dissatisfaction. One must state a clear purpose and continue in accordance with those stated aims. Betsy showed by her extreme behavior that she was determined not to live in a marriage that lacked co-operation by refusing to accept his behavior. However she never verbally specified why she was angry. She thought it was obvious but, often what is obvious to a female, is not to a male. She could have said, "Pay attention. I'm doing a strip for you."

Betsy showed Andrew what she did not like about his actions by emulating them. She might have also commented that she was illustrating his appearance of coldness. However, since she did not do this, Andrew turned the tables and playfully acted-out an identical characterization after he'd had time to contemplate what Betsy was signaling with her behavior.

Humor, respect for each other as an adult, sharing the work and love, brought a joyful reunion.

Let's hope that Betsy and Andrew will learn to mutually express their demands and wants in more nonthreatening ways which will bring harmony to their life.

Betsy represents the sexually frustrated woman who feels rejected and abandoned. This chapter's humorous reframing, hopefully, will release tension as it identifies a significant problem.

Chapter 12 is another illustration for contemplation. While some men sublimate their sex drive, others, such as Suffrin, in Chapter 12, sex escalates. Sally, his wife, has her own unique double-dealing methods of handing this. Sally has an attention-getting hook. Then she listens carefully to Suffrin's attitude and responds to it. Peruse this (sitcom type) chapter for applicable ways to create improved relationships within your home.

CHAPTER 12
SEX, SEX, AND MORE SEX

(Frogs keep proliferating. Will it never end?)

Suffrin wants to hug, kiss, and be sexual all the time. He continually tells his wife Sally, "I love you." He wants to do it right side up, upside down, and twisted like a pretzel. His penis is turned on high. He places his wife's hand over it so that she can appreciate her power over him.

Suffrin wants to do it on the kitchen table, on the living room floor, in the shower, in their car and van, under the stars upon the grass, and of course in their bed.

He passionately embraces her, and when their mouths meet Sally gasps for air. Each time he walks by her, he extends his arm to caress her breasts or pinch her buttock. The topic of conversation is sex, and how to do it better, and more sex.

Meanwhile Sally is hugged, pushed, pulled, poked, fondled, and thrown aside. Here's Sally's perception of her experience:

Sally is carefully mixing flour with grease to make a smooth consistency of gravy. The puppy is shredding newspapers while leaping to avoid the spatula that the baby is waving and banging indiscriminately. Sally looks back to avoid stepping on her infant son. Her foot lands instead on the edge of a pot that the baby had pulled from the cupboard. The handle swings upward hitting her shins. She slides across the room on the newspaper shreds and doubles over the sink. Next, she skids back, limping, in order to rescue the burned and lumpy gravy. She picks up the pot and screeches, "When am I going to remember to use a pot holder?" Dumps the contents in the sink, rinses her fingers with cold water, shakes her hands of the excess,

then scrubs the now blackened pan.
She measures the ingredients for more
gravy and begins again.

Enter-Romeo:

Saffron rushes in from behind. (He's
thought of his approach all day and he's
ready!) He plunges his hand deftly
under her bra and gently massages his
wife breasts.

Fireworks! Sally would love to respond
to his advances, but Suffrin has
interrupted her during work-time. Who
will watch the baby? Who will make the
supper? These thoughts took less than
a millionth of a second. So
instantaneous were they that Sally
forgot that she thought them as she
erupts, "Can't you see I'm busy?" The
frustration of being expected to sexually
participate during her work schedule
funneled into immediate anger.

Suffrin took on the little boy demeanor
of innocence, "You never have time for
me anymore. You're always busy. I'm
your puppet. You pull my strings.

Whenever you're ready, I'm supposed to be there."

Sally said, "If you were my puppet you'd be in a heap in the corner until I picked you up again. I'm your toy that you enjoy when you wish, and throw away when you're through."

"I'm not happy."

"I'm not responsible for your happiness."

"I'm not satisfied with our sex life. I try to keep it outrageously consuming."

"Try some other hobbies that don't include my participation. I'm tired of being a play thing."

"I'm not satisfied."

"I'm not satisfied, sometimes, either, but you roll over and go to sleep. I have to deal with that without your help."

"Why did I get married if you don't want sex with me?"

"Why indeed! Is that all I am? A convenient-sex partner? How did marriage make me suddenly a mirror image of your likes, dislikes, and appetites? My appetite is effected by daily events. I need a friend who understands that sliding in the dog's doo, watching Junior, burning my hand, and making dinner all simultaneously does not improve my sexual appetite.

"Pick up the baby. Clean up the mess around me, and discuss the news of the day. Let's be companions."

"I don't know what you're talking about." Suffrin really doesn't comprehended.

"I just spoke to a wall. How can I break through?" Sally turned towards the wall and began to address her comments to it, "I know you're hurting. You feel rejected when all your desires aren't met. I can't accept feeling guilty for your unmet drives. You'll have to find some ways to improve your life and give yourself direction. I want you to understand that I'm a person, and also have some unmet needs."

Throughout this speech, Suffrin's jaw was hanging ajar, his eyes were wide with horror. When he found words, he said, "Have you gone crazy? You were speaking to the wall!"

"I know. I get the same response from the wall as I get from you. But at least this time, I got your attention. I know when I have to turn you down, you feel abandoned. You are so needy. I'm exhausted trying to fulfill your demands. I feel as if I'm a Raggedy Ann doll".

"I feel like Raggedy Andy!"

"Great! Two dolls that can't move or speak who are trying to help each other. Let's go for marital counseling!"

"We shouldn't wash our dirty linen in public. I wouldn't know what to say anyway."

"That is such outdated reasoning. The TV talk shows illustrate how men have been conditioned from childhood to keep things to themselves. Their teachers, peers and relatives have told them. "Take it like a man and go on. Don't whine about it." Men get the message that they're not allowed to acknowledge gentle sensitive feelings. Their only release is sex and anger."

Suddenly Sally had some insight, "You feel lost when I'm not there to be your playmate, don't you? "

"I don't know."

"Well I'll bet you have a hollow feeling inside your stomach."

"Yes I do."

"Your feeling rejected. Tell me about it next time. Don't act on it." (Sally had just told their child, Billy, the same thing when he clung to her while she was cleaning. Billy had cried for her attention. "If you cry. I'll ignore you. Tell me want you want" Billy said, "Hugs-hugs." Sally had hugged him and said, "Now I have hugged you. I must get work done." Billy had persisted to cling.

Then, Sally had put him to bed with a kiss and then returned to her duties.)

Sally continued to instruct her husband, "Don't sneak up on me when you arrive home. I'll turn off the stove for five minutes, we'll embrace, then I'll resume cooking. Instead of watching TV, tonight, what say we converse!" Sally laughed.

Suffrin followed her suggestion. During supper, Sally recounted her hilarious, but exhausting day. She requested Suffrin view his day as if it were a T.V. comedy.

After many starts and slops, Suffrin began to connect with the funny events of his day, "John was standing on the scaffolding one story high, his hammer fell on the hard hat below. Tony wasn't hurt, but he swore, as he jumped five feet high. We could have played an Indian war tune, boom-boom, boom boom-boom, to the dance he was doing." Suffrin slapped the table. He hopped up and began a war dance, tapping his hand rhythmically, making the ooohs from his mouth a staccato.

Billy waddled in copying his father's actions. Sally and Suffrin's eyes met with pride and mutual caring. They all playfully tussled each other on the living room floor.

This is the beginning of a new relationship. If I can only keep the momentum going, Sally thought, we'll build a friendship that romance can only enhance.

Sally engaged Suffrin by challenging him to reframe his unpleasant day into a laughable situation. This decreased Suffrin's stress. Their infant, Billy related to the relaxed family ambience. Children quickly adopt new coping and language skills.

Sally will build a permanent close relationship, as long as, she continues her attentive communications laced with wit.

Here are some further suggestions for relationship enhancement:

1. Obtain the attention of the target person with whom you wish to develop a consensus of opinion. (Sally did this by immediately addressing the situation.)

2. Let the person know you are serious.

3. Hold your ground and offer creative solutions. This begins to improve the situation. (Sally offered additional information by referencing her remarks from TV shows.)

4. Active and accurate verbalizing of another's pain diffuses a tense situation. (Sally expressed how she felt sexy, then angry because she was unable to comply with his wishes which mirrored her own). Males are frequently out of touch with their own emotions. In the future Suffrin might be more able to identify his feelings.

It is important to understand and verbalize your males subconscious motives. Males range the human emotional gamut, just as much as females. Therefore, in order to cope with the cultural dictate to not appear mawkish, a majority of males have developed a suit of armor that denies them access to their own affections and those of others; awarding them with appellations of insensitive and immature brutes.

5. Refuse to accept the responsibility or the guilt for another's desires. This will keep the relationship on an adult level.

6. Be specific with demands and present alternative solutions. This helps to clarify the results. (Sally simplified the problem by creatively deciding to limit the embracing to five minutes while she interrupted her cooking).

7. Look for and restructuring unpleasant situations into humorous ones creates laughter which releases tension and creates a feeling of closeness.

A belly laugh engages the somatic system, It is a pleasant workout: It activates the muscular system, so that your legs are unable to support your weight and also uses the respiratory system as you breathe deeply.

Try it!:

HA HA HA HA HAH HEE HEE HEE HURUMP HURUMP HURUMP , HA HA HA HA HA HA, HOO HOO HOO HOO HOO HURUMP HURUMP HURUMP. Continue until you feel very warm and your cheeks are brick red. This invigorates your circulatory system. Tears run down your checks. Your sides hurt. You slide to the floor, rolling from side to side. Your neurological system is totally activated into supplying the neurotransmitters that transpose tension into peace.

The shared moment becomes very precious. A bridge has spanned the emptiness between you and another. What a beautiful way to build a marriage!

(And they are on their way to becoming Royalty.)

In the next Chapter 13, women attempt to build relationship bridges. Women often therapeutically play "Can you top this?" Women offer each other solutions and quips while commiserating over their spouse's immature˘ behaviors. Women learn from each other's experiences. The danger in marriages is that when women are also immature, both sexes are stuck as frogs instead of royalty.

CHAPTER 13

UNITED WE STAND

(You decide from these personalized conversations Frogs or Royalty?) If they mirror your life, perhaps you need to consider some revisions in your life?

Females often use each other to vent, gather information and resolve communal issues. Here is such a gathering:

Mary, Marjorie, and Cecil munch lunch at their favorite restaurant. Cecil, a tall, slender, blonde in a pink business suit is speaking. "John insists I go with him to buy a suit," Mary's brown eyes glistened as she leaned forward. She carefully held her sleeve of her black dress up over the food as she pointed, as if, to accentuate the area she was demarcating, "Have you ever noticed in the men's department, the men always have their wives along?" Dark complexioned Marjorie's intense hazel eyes swept from Mary to Cecil "David wanted me to bring him home shoes! Can you imagine? All the lasts are different with each manufacturer. How could I get him the right size?"

"A friend of mine said she always purchased her husbands entire wardrobe, including shoes. I asked her how she did it. She said that she brought home several sizes and then returned the incorrect ones the next day," Cecil said. The group gasped and tittered. "Mom used to say that she had four babies. The three of us kids and Dad. I know what she's talking about now," Cecil spoke in a conspiracy tone of voice. "John gets the kids going as soon as he comes in the front door. He tickles them until they are screaming. They sit down to dinner all red-faced and sweaty. The children. can't go to sleep, and up chuck from the strenuous wrestling matches."

Mary nodded, her brown curls danced up and down, "I'd the same problems with Al, so I fed the kids early and put them to bed before he got home. Then he and I have some quiet time, too.

He questioned me as to why they were already in bed, so I told him. He liked the new arrangement, but requested that I put them to bed after he'd a chance to see them. I told him I'd agree as long as he'd only read them stories or talk quietly with them. He agreed. Mary Jane doesn't have nightmares anymore, I've noticed. I never connected the rough play to her terrified nights until the roughhousing stopped."

Cecil leaned forward enthusiastically, "You can't put eight and nine-year-old's to bed at six pm. John and I want to maintain the family unit. Dinner is the only time when we can all be together before everyone goes their own way. Peter and Karen have to do their homework. John goes into the garage to fix the car, or build his current airplane model. I've got to clean up and make sandwiches for the next day."

Mary pressed her mouth into a raised lump, "When is it our turn to rest?"

"At these luncheons!" Marjorie eyebrows raised as if to accentuate her comments.

"Yes, but all we do is complain about out male-adolescents instead of enjoying ourselves." Mary said. The group laughed at themselves, but continued their bellyaching.

Marjorie absentmindedly flicked a crumb off her yellow suit-skirt as she said, "Why is it that our husbands give us money to buy ourselves our own gifts, but they want to be surprised with presents that fit their exact prescriptions.? I ran from store to store trying to find an outdated jacket because it's the only kind he'll wear. I was lucky. I located a business upstate that had stuff from the year one. He loved it."

Mary's eyes shone as she said, "Next Christmas give him a package with cash in it and see if he thinks it's great!"

"Great idea!" Cecil's forehead wrinkled, "But would you do it?" She brushed back the lock of hair that had escaped from her neat coiffure.

"I guess it depends on how vindictive I feel next year," Marjorie flippantly said, "'I don't like holding on to resentment."

Cecil leaned forward intently, ""Why is it when we are vindictive it is labelled catty, but acceptable when a male does it? The only way our men are going to know how we hurt, is by letting them experience the same situation."

"I think I'd rather purchase my own gift and let him purchase his. We could gift wrap our own. I think I'll suggest that to David next time. It's is a gentler way to get him to understand that a surprise is more fun," Marjorie said.

"And romantic," Cecil said with a wry grin. She rolled her eyes to suggest the facetiousness of her comments" Yes that would really do it for my John!" She burst out laughing. "He wouldn't get the picture at all!"

Mary ignored Cecil's remarks and responded to the gist of Marjorie's comments. "Do you know what I think would be the most romantic thing Al could do?"

"Just once putting on a wash without telling me that it's woman's work." Mary had a sly smirk on her round face.

"What?," her two friends joined in-in unison.

Cecil said, " You're easy to please!" She continued, "The men hide behind gender roles to get out of work. John claims he doesn't know how to use the appliances. That's ridiculous! I've shown him how. He can read directions just as well as I can! Then he ruined my good white dress by putting it in with his red parka."

"Just like kids, they ruin things so we'll stop asking them to share the work," Marjorie grimaced. Her glance encompassed the room as if she were asking the customers to agree with her.

Well we won't let them get away with it, will we? We'll keep the heat on," Mary snickered. She sat more erectly in the chair.

Cecil had other things on her mind, "John only wants steak and potatoes. The budget's tight. Food is the only place I can cut. The mortgage company won't accept that I can't fit them into my budget."

"For heaven's sake! Speak to John about it. But then. Can you afford this luncheon?" Marjorie looked into Cecil's finely chiseled face with concern.

"Why should I watch every penny when he won't make sacrifices?" Cecil flashed a look of annoyance towards the group. She brought her shoulders up and then down as she sighed with frustration. Cecil was looking for the groups loyal backing and hadn't expected them to emphasize her frailties.

Marjorie recognized that she had let down Cecil's expectations. She said,

"My friend, Carol had the same problem. She gave her husband one third of a steak each night. He wanted to know where the rest of the dinner was? She told him that Kelly was wearing it on her feet. Jack said, "She's wearing steaks on her feet?" Then Carol said, "With what I'm saving by serving you less steak, I was able to buy Kelly the shoes she needed for school." He said he didn't know that things were that bad and he went over the budget with her after supper." Doesn't Carol have an amusing way to get her point across?"

"Al wouldn't respond that way!" Mary was exasperated. "He won't eat vegetables. Our Mary Jane says, 'I don't have to eat veggies cause Daddy doesn't.'"

Cecil inquired, "How old is Mary Jane now?"

"She's almost two. Mary Jane and Joey imitate their Daddy. He's their God. Whatever he does must be right."

Marjorie expanded her rotund bust and began her tirade, "Men have their own set of rules. They are entitled to the best food, a night out with the guys, to watch TV when they're tired. Last week I was so sick. Diarrhea. Vomiting. I could barely hang on until David got home. I'd made supper and had it on the table for him when he walked in. He rushed past me and said, 'I'm too sick to eat. I'm going straight to bed.' I couldn't believe it! I had to stay up until I put the kids to bed," She continued, "But when he is sick, he wants to be entertained! I'm supposed to drop everything and talk to him because he's lost interest in TV."

"In stressful overworked times I think of our ancestors extended family groups. Someone, an aunt or a grandmother would take over," Mary said. "However, I guess it had its drawbacks. Al's family eat junk food constantly. I'd never break my kids of that habit if they lived with his family."

Mary returned the conversation to Marjorie's comments, "Marjorie, I'm glad you waited until we'd finished our appetizer before accounting the disgusting details of your virus with us. But since you did, I'll share my toilet lesson with all of you."

"Quit kidding us. You'd tell us your obnoxious story regardless of whether I'd told mine."

The three close friends laughed knowing that they could commensurate any part of their lives. They had met in grade school. The long association had become a sibling-type-relationship.

"Well, anyway! The toilet plugged up and Al was turning green as he was plunging it. I thought it was a good time to tell him, that his arteries are just as disgustingly plugged with cholesterol from all the fat, salt, and sugar junk foods he eats. It really worked! Al changed his diet. He's sleeping well and doesn't need Maalox anymore," Mary said.

Cecil said, "We're eating lunch here."
She changed the subject, "This lasagne
reminds me of the time John told me
that, if I could cook like his Mom did,
he'd eat it. I was one over on him
because his Mom had supervised every
ingredient that I added so I could
surprise John that night. I told him he
was a 'Mommy's boy' and was missing
his Mom-not her cooking.

Cecil continued, "It was his Mom's idea.
I told her all his complaints. She said,
'Why you cook as well as I, but I'll
oversee all you do if you wish today. If
he still complains then we'll know his
problem!' His Mom said that John
always had trouble accepting change.
She said that when he was fifteen years
old, John pestered to go to summer
camp all winter, but after she granted
him permission, he became upset and
never mentioned it again.'"

"The men that I know, have trouble
dealing with small changes in their
schedule," Marjorie said. She
continued, "Joan told me that when her

Joe wouldn't eat leftovers, she cooked him his meat and potatoes and made her own gourmet meals."

"I don't like leftovers either. What do you mean gourmet meals from leftovers?" Mary snorted her annoyance.

"Meat loaf, Hungarian goulash, chicken pot pies, are all second night meals. Right? They're delicious. They smell superb. Well, when Joe got the nightly aroma treat he was curious to try out the meals. Joan told him, 'You don't like leftovers, remember? I wouldn't dream of forcing you to eat them.' Joan wouldn't give him a sample,'" Marjorie said.

"Joan's too much!" Mary threw her head back and chuckled.

Marjorie continued, "The next night she served him leftovers. She said that he never said a word. He's been eating them ever since!"

"I guess I should tear a page from her book! I fixed pork chops the first week we were married. John said that he wasn't going to eat raw meat. I couldn't convince him that they were perfect. So I proceeded to cook them until they were stiff! I told John that's the next stage after well done. Instead of it working out for me as it did for Joan, he constantly tells me what a lousy chef I am. He makes fun of me in front of company," Cecil said.

"You get too hot under the collar. Ignore him and he'll stop making an issue of it. Better yet. Tell him since he doesn't like your cooking, he can be chef from now on. That ought to dampen his teasing," Marjorie enjoyed giving advice.

Mary crinkled her forehead in thought, "Did you ever notice how men complain about things and then leave us to solve the problem?"

Cecil laughed, "I wonder what they would do if we didn't take the bait?"

"Let's make a pact. The next time our husbands dump a problem they should solve in our laps, we'll allow it to lie there until they do something about it!" Marjorie was leading the revolution again.

"I'll second the motion," Mary raised her pudgy hand.

"Yeah. Sounds good to me," Cecil said.

The waitress refilled the coffee cups as the friends conversed.

Marjorie the cheerleader of the group entered her major complaint of the day, "What bothers me the most is when men illogically blame us for things that are beyond our control. David was angry because his car broke down on our corner and how dare I not have x-ray vision to see through our house so that I would know to and come out and give him a hand!"

"Boy do I know that one! Al blamed me because the wind ripped the door from my hands and sprang the hinges on the car door," Mary heatedly said.

"John said I was stupid, because I didn't pick up his suit from the dry cleaners. Yet he never mentioned that he took it there. So how could I know to pick it up. I'd have to check with him daily for his activities. I don't have the time for that," Cecil said.

Marjorie answered her own question of how to deal with dilemma, she said, "We'll have to respond the next time we're expected to be swamis 'We'll enroll in psychic courses today.'" The group laughed.

"That takes care of that type of illogical reasoning. What about when you ask your husband to be responsible for selling the car and he does nothing about it for months at a time? Al put only one add in the paper. He thinks the car will advertise itself? When I asked him to place another add, he responded by telling me that he'd get rid of it by taking it to the dump." Mary was clearly exasperated.

"Dump him," Cecil said with exuberance.

Marjorie was contemplating this perplexing problem. "Obviously he feels that you're overloading his life. Maybe we should all chip in and buy him a playpen?"

Mary said. "Oh be real!". .

"I'll place the add myself. It's not worth the aggravation," Cecil said.

"He's counting on that!" Mary said.

"Oh,well. We can't win them all," Marjorie readied herself to leave. The others pushed back their chairs, and put on their coats. "We'll solve the world problems, next week same time, same place?" Mary and Cecil nodded. They all left smiling.

Group gathering such as this luncheon, benefit women by giving them a gripe session that allows them to let off steam that might otherwise be directed toward their spouses. The group offers unprofessional therapy by offering many alternatives to comparable frustrating situations.

These are people's opinions which must be factored into your decision as to whether or not to follow their ideas. Any intuitive feelings that these are not right for you, should be discussed with a relationship counselor.

People need to realize that they do not suffer alone. What they had previously regarded as 'my unique burden' becomes common place and therefore, manageable. The group's creative solutions may or may not apply to their situation, but they learn that there are many approaches to an issue. They might find an entirely revolutionary outcome. More importantly the group provides the active empathetic listening that women require in order to dissipate the emotional baggage that accumulated.

Some additional methods to improve incompatible situations are suggested here:

Take a circumstance that infuriates you and write a list of possible responses that you could make and the possible reactions of your husband. Now create another list of your own possible responses to his.

Study your reactions. Now make a list of comments on why you will or will not utilize some of your retorts.

Is your choice of a solution based on fear of what your mate will do or say? Is that terror based on reality or anxiety stemming from a traumatic happening in your background or in your marriage? Or are you merely unwilling to hear his annoyance or put up with his reactions?

Do you feel that women should not act so assertively? Do you feel that women should not state what they like? (If your response is yes, you are saying then that women are not entitled to have preferences). If that is the case, you are buying into the Traditional Role that women should be retiring, nurturing and yielding.

Do you feel uncomfortable because you see yourself as retiring and non-assertive? Study men's reactions. Are they assertive? Do they feel they have rights? Why are you taking your rights away from yourself? if you haven't the freedom to speak up, then neither should your partner have that privilege. Notice what a man asserts as his rights. Ask yourself why you are not allowing yourself the same standards. When we play a game of monopoly everyone plays by the same rules. Only the eleven year old feels that the rules should not apply to him and the youth changes them to suit his purpose. We stop playing with him because we want him to mature and discover that the rules must be the same for everyone or it isn't a fair game.

Make your game of life fair. Equalize the rules.

The next Chapter 14, extensively uses farcical restructuring to illustrate improvements. (This tongue in check escapade is not meant to be taken literally). However comedy can be the soap and water that can begin to cleanse and repair hurts.

As a counselor, I use stories to identify and objectify situations in order that clients may view themselves from a different perspective. Outlandish accounts help them to laugh at themselves. When distrust rears its ugly head, suggesting absurd alternatives aids in reframing issues.

Chapter 14, is a comedic account which illustrates how reality may be misinterpreted An analogous situation happened to me many years ago, but the trust in the relationship prevented it from escalating.

CHAPTER 14

COMEDY OF ERRORS

(Or froggy terrors?)

This story accentuates how to deal with misunderstandings in a burlesque manner.

It all began when Laura became a godparent to her niece. Laura and Bob agreed

to baby-sit Marion, which they felt which would bring the families closer. When they had children (Laura was pregnant) they could relieve each other to have free time as a couple. When the time came for Laura and Bob to do it, Bob decided that this was a great chance for him to join the boys for a drink. Since Bob was partying he felt it best to stay overnight with Fred, one of his single friends, so that he wouldn't get a DWI driving home. Laura was left to spend an uneventful evening alone on a very lumpy couch at her sister's house. This had become a once a month ritual and each time the lumps became more uncomfortable as Laura grew in size. Each month Bob had a single night out with the guys, ending with an overnight stay at his best friends house.

Laura was beginning to resent Bob's manipulation of what was supposed to be more time spent together as a couple. It was now, for her, more time spent alone. Her sister Barbara and her brother-in-law Calvin seemed to be the only ones benefiting from this arrangement. One night, Laura had the perfect excuse to call her hubby, the weather had suddenly turned bitter and she hadn't worn a coat. She phoned Bob at Fred's house at two in the morning and found them in good spirits. He said, "No I can't pick you up now. I'm feeling woozy, but I'll stop by our house in the morning and get your coat." With that, Laura tried to bed down on the even lumpier- feeling couch. Laura placed the couch pillows on the floor, recoiling from side to side in an effort to feel comfortable. Calvin and Barbara had frequently invited her to join them in their bed during those overnight stays. Laura felt that was an inappropriate thing to do. Barbara had argued with a twinkle in her eyes, "I'll sleep in between, so there's no orgy going on here!" Laura had never shared this conversation with her spouse because she had dismissed the possibility of it ever happening from her mind. However, tonight with growing physical discomfort she crawled into the crowded-regular size bed. It was already three a.m. and the three slept deeply until they were awakened at ten a.m. by the door bell.

Barbara arose and pulled the curtain aside, that separated the bedroom from the living room, as she went to answer the apartment door. Bob entered, dropped the coat on the couch and glanced towards the bedroom. Calvin and Laura smiled sleepily at Bob from the bed.

"Hi Honey. Did you bring me my coat?"

Bob had an incredulous look on his face. He reddened. Then, he plunged out the door, slamming it. Barbara, Calvin, and Laura exchanged glances as they began to howl. Barbara sat on the side of the bed, "He thought-he thought," her voice trailed off as she gestured wordlessly towards the door.

"This isn't funny! But did you see his look?" with that Laura's laughter sounded like a machine gun patter. The three tried to be serious but the demeanor only created more roguish hysteria. The convulsions began with holding their sides, and then grabbing each other. Each serious effort created more levity. Barbara, Laura, and Calvin were now roaring on the bed, ball-like. All three clung to each other as they guffawed. Barbara heard the door and drew away just seconds before Bob's appearance once again caught Laura and Bob in bed-but this time in a clinch.

Laura giggled herself into labour. Within the next fifteen minutes while the baby was prematurely presenting itself, Laura alternately; tittered chuckled, chortled, shrieked, and howled.

During the next few weeks, Bob developed a steel-like silence about the incident which prevented Laura from explaining what really happened. Obviously, Laura and Barbara concurred that Bob would never be able to relate to the innocence of the happenstance unless

they turned the tables on him. They decided on a plan of action which would have to wait until several incidents occurred simultaneously.

A month later the scheme was perfect for enactment. Laura had a friend's shower to attend. Bob stayed home with his infant son. It was a stormy night. Laura called Barbara from the bride to be's house. Then Barbara parked one block from her brother-in-law's house. She raced through the storm, timing her movements so that they would synchronize with Laura's watch. She rang the doorbell and pushed by Bob as he opened the door. She was a large woman so her request of letting her put on his house coat so she could get out of the soaked clothes sounded very reasonable.

Meanwhile Laura had driven home, turned off the motor about a half a block from the house, turned off the car lights and pulled close to the curb as she let the car roll to a stop outside the first-floor-apartment. Laura waited for the bedroom light to click off/on three time, letting her know that Barbara was alerting her to barge in on them. Barbara would wait until she heard Laura open the door and then she would walk out the bedroom door into the living room in Bob's housecoat, as planned. They timed it perfectly.

Bob didn't expect Laura to return for several hours. He looked up, then gawked first at Laura and then at Barbara who continued into the room with bare feet and his garment wrapped around her. Bob said, "This isn't what it looks like."

"'Yeah? Tell me about it?" Barbara acted out the part well. She even sneered.

He began to stutter. "Your sister's car broke down and she got soaked walking over here." Laura smirked.

"What could I do? Your clothes won't fit her."

"Looks bad doesn't it?" Laura sternly said.

A few moments later, Laura and Barbara began explosively laughing. Bob had disbelief in his voice. He gulped air. He looked from Laura to Barbara trying to discern what was transpiring, "This was a set-up?"

Laura and Barbara nodded, chortling, "You wouldn't let us tell you what happened the night the baby was born so we decided if you'd experience it you'd realize it was just a set of innocent circumstances."

"But you were in bed with Calvin." He looked at his wife. His eyebrows were raised. His eyes nearly crossed.

Barbara said, "But I was in the middle all night until you knocked on the door. Laura had a restless night so I made sure I didn't wake her as I got out of the bed."

"Barbara convinced me to sleep next to her. The couch was lumpy. I was uncomfortable."

Of course! The baby was almost due! I never for a moment believed that anything was going on."

"Oh no! of course you didn't." Laura and Barbara said in unison as they looked at each other and cackled.

Another melee of pealing laughter, and lack of muscular co-ordination transpired. Calvin walked in and found them all frolicking on the floor. He stood perplexed and then said, "You'll tell me latter. Right?" They nodded. Calvin was drawn into the jubilant spirit. Latter, everyone was enlightened about all the details.

Many objectives are accomplished with this story:

1. Laura discovers that Bob has utilized his male-mandate in order to carve out more freedom for himself, by changing their agreement midstream, so that he could have entire evenings out.

Women frequently don't perceive this shift that allows two sets of rules; his and hers. Unilateral decisions which reverse contractual verbal agreements can only be honored if one party allows the other party to make and break the original rules. Women frequently allow men to do exactly that-without even being aware-that they give men unlimited freedom. Women limit their own freedom. The one sided decision of Bob's to party alone while his wife baby-sat all alone was a reversal of the previous arrangement in order that they could spend more time together after their child was born.

Women are so accustomed to yielding that it never occurs to them that they have allowed themselves to become a welcome mat. The man comes home, wipes his feet at the door, and leaves all marital responsibility there with the dirt.

Bob side-tracked Laura from her objections about his going out with the guys with reassurances that staying at Fred's would prevent a DWI. The manipulation, as in the majority of homes, channels into another issue. The original issue of a broken verbal contract gets lost, as the unrelated issue is argued. In many cases such as in this story there was not an argument, but a gullible acceptance of the entire diversion. (But then women are supposed to be gullible according to the Traditional role.)

Bob's lack of communication prevented any access toward clearing up the misunderstanding.

Laura and Barbara used an analogous situation to help Bob break the silent barricade. Their apprehension sparked a laughter reaction which brought all of them closer because it relieved the tension. Guffawing brought deep breathing, increased blood flow, and relaxed the body muscles so that the participants were no longer able to support their body weight. These physical reactions break-up the bodily tension.

Bob was having difficulties with the value called trust. It is difficult to believe that truth is more unbelievable than fiction. Laura and Barbara intuitively acknowledged that a different form of communication was required, because communication was extinguished by Bob's silent edict. They enacted a parable so that he could emotionally accept the reality. People can accept the logic, but that doesn't convince their ego. The distrust stems from our sense of morality and our emotional reactions to it. These areas of our brain are chemical reactions which are termed neurotransmitters by scientists. Since the female's three ego states (logic, morality, and emotions) work within a different priority system from those of men, we women need to co-ordinate them in order to feel whole again. For example women need an affirmation of their feelings, then everything else falls into place. Men place a higher emphasis on facts. Understanding this glitch commences the start of a communication bridge between the sexes.

Calvin asked for and patiently waited for an explanation. Since he took this approach, his subconscious was freed to piece together all the circumstances. Therefore, Calvin didn't require an elaborate scenario to awaken his awareness. Communication is the most efficient when it is verbal. Then hurt feelings, and misunderstandings are immediately cleared, instead of festering for long periods of time. However, if everyone were that organized you wouldn't have the fun of watching or reading comedy cases such as these.

Most of the fun in life is laughing at ourselves and our limitations. Maybe we shouldn't improve? Try viewing the upsetting situation as if it were a play on TV. Is it now more capricious?

I'll leave you to decide whether the next fictionalized hilarious Chapter 15 is identifiable to your situation.

Many men, the culture, and the I.R.S. labels a woman who is not a paid employee, but works exclusively at home. A housewife has become synonymous with unemployed. Unemployed means not working! Is it true that housewives watch T.V. all day

long? Tune into Chapter 15 for one day
in the life of a housewife for the answer!

CHAPTER 15
ONE EXOTIC DAY IN THE LIFE OF A HOUSEWIFE

There are still some (frog) men who don't view housework as work. Some housewives also share that perspective. I suggest women write down the time and the work that is accomplished during that time span. I have had women amazed by how much they do!

If this is not an issue for you, you might want to skip this chapter.

Bored by the mundaneness of housewife duties, Jessica entertains herself with an imaginary affair. (Matthew is her imaginary perfect man. Jim is her husband.)

The door bell rang. Standing at the door was the most gorgeous man that Jessica had ever seen. "My name is Matthew," he said as he entered.

Matthew was everything Jessica wanted a man to be. He treated Jessica respectfully, listening intently to all her comments. "I agree that romance is more than a bedtime approach. It is, for me at least, a time to share all our thoughts with each other," Matthew's voice resonated through her. Her heart raced, and her body-heat soared. He said, "Everything you say Is important to me. How was your. day today?"

"Boring. Everyday is the same as the day before. The kitchen floor gets dirty within minutes of scrubbing it." The only variation is that some days, I wash the windows in lieu of the floor. I don't want to talk about it. It makes me yawn."

"Of course the repetitious activities makes a bright person like you feel dull."

Jessica felt beautiful. Matthew understood the drudgery of housework She was very responsive to his stroking her hair.

The smell of her hair, the litheness of her body was more than Matthew could stand.

Matthew was a mythical perfect counterpart to Jessica's daily life. Some day when she finds a spare moment she might make it a book. However, she barely has time for the log-entries that she is composing in order to show Jim, her husband, how much time is utilized for each ordinary task. Jim remarked this morning before going to work that it would be nice if she did something today besides coffee klatch. Therefore, Jessica had begun a daybook to show Jim. Frankly Jessica didn't feel she accomplished much of anything either.

Here are her entries:

MORNING 6:00-6:15 A.M. Showered.

6:15-6:20 A.M.
Brushed teeth and accomplished other toiletry items.

6:20-6:50 A.M.
Prepared breakfast, bacon, eggs, toast, put out the cereal.

6:50-6:53 A.M. Awoke Jim.

6:53-7:08 A.M.

Ate breakfast with Jim.

7:08-7:13 A.M.

Prepared sandwich for Jim's lunch, wrapped it, poured coffee into vacuum, placed the contents into a lunch box.

7:13-7:15 A.M.
Kissed Jim good-bye, handed him his lunch.

(Jessica is trying to maintain the loving relationship, that has been cooling, by kissing Jim when he departs.)

7:16 A.M.
Baby Julia has been crying and calling out since 7:08 to be picked up and changed.

(Jessica feels guilty for not immediately attending to her, but Jim has a time schedule that must be met, so Julia has to wait her turn.)

7:16-8:00 A.M.

Wash baby and play with her.

(Jessica read child-developmental books during her pregnancy. She knows the importance of spending quality time helping her child relate socially to the world, knowing that the stimulus will increase her mental capabilities in school.)

8:00-8:05 A.M. Diapered Julia.

8:05-8:10 A.M.
Made one bed. Stripped the wet sheets from the crib.

8:10-8:12
Julia wandered into another room. Brought her back where I can watch her.

8:12-8:17 A.M.
Gathering laundry and placing it in the hamper.

8:17-9:17 A.M.
Picking up after Jim and myself. Put dishes, papers, letters, clothes all in the proper places.

9:17-9:25 A.M.

Picking up the newspapers that Julia
was shredding all over the house while
I was picking up. Stuffing newspapers
into bags.

9:25-9:30 A.M.
Diaper change and kissing Julia.

9:30-10-45 A.M.

Swept and mopped kitchen floor, rinsed
dishes, placed in the dish washer,
wiped off the counters and kitchen
table, unloaded dish washer and put
dishes and silverware away. Julia
pulled all the clean pots out and banged
them on the floor. Rewashed the frying
pans and pots that Julia dirtied by
playing with on the floor, then dried
them. Put them away. Julia screamed
for attention. I comforted her. Noticed
that the milk container leaked all over
the refrigerator shelves. Cleaned it.

10:45-11:35 A.M.

Defrosted the refrigerator. Checking on
Julia from time to time to make certain

that she isn't into an electric outlet or pulling the phone off the hook.

11:35-12:00 A.M.
Prepared lunch for Julia and myself.

AFTERNOON 12:00-12:18 P.M.

Ate lunch with Julia and talked with her. Tried to teach her to say words.

12:18-12:30 P.M.

Cleared and cleaned the table. Swept the floor of the remains that Julia spilled as she ate. Washed up the few dishes by hand, dried them, put them away as Julia played behind me. I have to watch each time I step back so that I don't step on her.

12:30-1:30 P.M.

Dusted and polished the furniture throughout the house. Showed Julia how to use the spray. Her help messed up the effect. Had to redo it when she wasn't looking. (Repolishing the table in front of Julia would imply to Julia that she was not important. Jessica didn't want the child's self-esteem to be demeaned. Jessica knows a child learns through observation and practice.)

1:30-1:45 P.M.
Changed Julia's diaper again. Rocked her for a few minutes.

Jessica's imagination began again: Matthew swept Julia off her feet and nuzzled his face into her long hair. He gently placed her on the bed, undressing her as they conversed.

1:46 -1:50 P.M.
Put daughter in for a nap.

1:50-2:05 P.M.
Checked the bank statement. Balanced the check book.

2:06-2:21 P.M.
Sorted clothes, checked for stains. Put clothes into the washer.

Matthew said, "Its great to be with you."

2:21-2:51 P.M.

Put things in proper places in the cellar. Washed down the appliances.

Matthew gently removed the rest of Julia's clothing.

2:51-2:59 P.M.

Removed laundry from the clothes washer, placed into the dryer. washing machine.

Matthew's hands swept across Julia's thighs.

2:59-3:40 P.M.
Continued to clean cellar. Swept floor.

Matthew nibbled Julia's ear.

3:40-4:00 P.M.

Put another load into the

Sorted, folded, put away clothes from first load from dryer, and placed in the proper drawers and closets.

(Jessica's imaginative lovemaking was interrupted by Jessica's intruding thoughts of Julia. Jessica checked the crib. Julia was still sleeping. Jessica tried to return to her imagination, but she felt as if she were cheating on Jim. So she envisioned a second honeymoon in Hawaii. The mindless undemanding physical labour left her free to picture the palm trees gently swaying. The Hawaiian guitar melodies on the radio accompanied her as she visualized Jim and herself swimming in the crystal clear Pacific Ocean. Next, they were exchanging romantic glances as they danced clutched tightly. Julia's cries pulled Jessica from her reverie at 4:01 P.M.)

4:01-4:05 P.M.
Removed second load from the washer and placed into the dryer.

Jessica felt very upset that she was delaying Julia's cries for assistance but, she wanted to complete the task that she was doing without having the baby pull all the folded clothes out of the basket and run playfully away with them as she had in the past. Jessica knew that the five minute task could easily become thirty minutes with the type of help a two-year-old child can give.)

4:05-4:15 P.M.
Comforted baby. Changed diaper. Showed Julia how to put wooden puzzle pieces together.

EARLY EVENING AND EVENING

4:15-6:15 P.M.
Drove to and from supermarket. Shopped, packed and unpacked car of groceries.

"Where's my sweetheart," Matthew said, as he arrived home at his usually five o'clock hour. "It's wonderful to have you home. Some men get in at such late hours."

(Julia helped her mom shop by pulling items Jessica didn't want onto the floor. Jessica had to grab the items so they wouldn't break and put them back. Julia was insulted so she screamed. Jessica wanted to crack her but, contained herself while the items were going through the check-out counter. Then

Jessica put the screaming infant into the car first, next loading her groceries in the trunk. Jessica was feeling tired and frazzled.)

Brought groceries into house Put them into proper places: refrigerator, cupboards etc.

6:15-7:25 P.M.

Washed and peeled potatoes and carrots. Diced same. Whipped up a biscuit mix and put aside. Pulled chicken off of the bones, diced same. Opened can of soup and used as gravy and placed all in oven with biscuit mix on top for chicken pot pie. Popped Mrs. Smith's pre- made apple pie in oven with it.

Cleaned up boxes, utensils, and dishes used in the food preparation. places.

7:25-7:31 P.M.
Changed a messy diaper.

7:31-7:35 P.M.
Sitting to drink a cup of coffee.

Put same in proper

(Jim slams the door behind him, "Is that all you do drink coffee all day long? I wish I had it so easy, where I could sit down whenever I wanted, like you do! I'm exhausted!"

7:35-7:50 P.M.
Setting the table, serving the food.)

7:50-8:00 P.M.
Cutting up Julia's food. Feeding her the last remains.

(Jim has nearly completed his meal.)

8:00-8:15 P.M. Eat my dinner.

8:15-8:35 P.M.

Sweep floor under Julia's chair. Clean up her high chair that is covered with food smears from her hands. Rinse dishes, place in dishwasher.

8:35-9:25 P.M.
Bathe Julia, undress and dress for bed, brush her teeth, read her bedtime stories.

9:25-10:00 P.M.

Make coffee, serve pie, eat, clean up mess. Take dishes from the dishwasher and put in cupboard.

(Jim watched TV from 8:00 P.M. until bedtime. Jim is now angry that Jessica is too tired to play in bed with him.)

But, today Jessica hands him her log. Jim reads it. His jaw drops open with amazement, "I guess I never realized how much you did! It does seem as though you could cut corners on some of this. Why don't you do the dishes and floor once a week?" Jessica bristled, "Now you're conducting my day for me! Remember you complained that the floor looked grimy? There are still odd jobs that are done infrequently such as washing the windows, cleaning the refrigerator and defrosting it."

"I'm trying to be helpful. I didn't see what you did all day. Now I know. Is every day like this?" Jim said.

Jessica smiled, "Some days are worse."

Counselor's comments:

It is best to keep a daily log for one month. A chronicle of the days events outlining the work details refutes the unemployed-myth by showing the actual facts of a taxing schedule. Even wives are amazed. The daily repetition of duties creates a state of demoralization. They are boring because of their inaneness which erases the housewife's significance as a person. Time sheets shared with the spouse facilitates co-operation and more respect as a human being.

(The working housewife/mother is respected for her salary contribution, nevertheless her day off is similar to Jessica's.) However the change of pace and the need to tightly schedule which job should take precedence allows little time for fantasizing. Both the homemaker and the career woman must illustrate to their husbands that household activities take time, even if they do not represent a high level of thinking. A housewife must organize efficiently regardless of the multiple distractions that children, telephones calls, and crises create. This planning is equivalent to a high powered executive position. Yet she accomplishes it with such ease that she gives herself no credit.

Therefore, training your husband is really learning to express yourself clearly so that the husband can relate to your needs. Clear communication which includes solid undeniable information, such as a log represents, overcomes stereotypical concepts.

(I offer the following theory): The cultural myth that women who are housewives don't work, has subliminally entered the culture through the Protestant work ethic which was: A person is good if they work. That ethic combined with the early successes of the original immigrants gave rise to wealth, which led the American public to link goodness, productivity, and money as one inseparable unit. Therefore, since the good wife contributes no money, it enters the subconscious group mentality that the she contributes no recognizable effort, ergo the myth: she does not work!

Her only payment for labour is her husband's and the culture's acknowledgement that It is work. (Work is defined as an obligation with has defined hours and duties.) You may comment that equality is already here. If it is, then why is the majority of women who frequent my office have full time outside employment, yet are still picking up the major responsibilities of housewife duties, mothering, accounting, shopping, etc., while her husband returns home to relax and decide to help when it suits his pleasure? She can not put her children on a shelf until she is rested and ready to feed, wash, bed them, or help them with homework, etc. Someone must do it . Some husbands chose not to share this responsibility. When a woman works full time, the so called women's work should be a shared male/female obligation.

Women say to me, "Why should I get stuck with all the work and then then be the only one putting an effort into the relationship?" I tell them, "You don't. You have the choice to walk out." I also say, "Try to gain your husband's co-operative effort. However, if you can't do this but, still want to have a good relationship, then you must develop various skills that will produce your wish.

The dynamics of change may be experienced through pleasant refraining such as mentioned throughout this book. Humorously restyling situations by identifying the cultural myths, the historical role models, becoming aware of the game-plays, and by presenting facts, feelings, and concepts in order to heighten the male's awareness of societal changes taking place around him so that novel perceptions and reactions can be advanced.

Some men, cannot identify with the equal rights concept, because they have always been equal. The constitution granted them that freedom. Not until the early nineteen-hundreds did women gain that same liberty. However, the privilege granted women has been limited by all of the above named restrictions of the preceding paragraph. Men have not had to fight these taboos, therefore, they are not aware they exist. If boundaries are subliminally imposed a male

can hardly be sympathetic. I find that women, are individually fighting a revolutionary battle on their individual and lonely terrain of marriage.

CHAPTER 16

IN THE SAME BOAT

(Frogs taking a ride?)

The bride and groom took the same vows which state they will divide life's burdens 50/50. Women understand that the vows signify equality. However men don't seem to know that. In many cases men believe it is more 150/50 their gain. (Some women take advantage of the new equality and make their efforts 50% and the men are doing 150%. Neither sex should take advantage of the other.)

Women are employed outside the home, inside the home, at the supermarket, caring for the kids, and in the last couple of generations have even taken on the couple's accounting. Seventeen hour days, seven day weeks are exhausting American women.

Immature men do not fathom the link between the depletion of female resources with lackluster lovemaking which then leads directly or indirectly to the divorce courts.

However, if women turn the tables and have the men do all the household and child care chores, then it is no longer an equal marriage. Equality works both ways.

Women who love heir husbands, realize that trading one boyish guy for another, doesn't improve the work load. they may as well work it out with the one they've got.

This group might try Humor to establish closeness, and to deliver the message that co-operative responsibilities are the order of the day (for those who have not understood that message yet).

Marriages, people find, are analogous to large buildings. The couple's marriage is in the same building, but the spouses are on different floors. Each partner is communicating ideas at his or her level but the layers in between prevents them from hearing

and understanding the concepts -
projected. Mirth is the telephone line
that translate the floors into one level.

Laughing together establishes
closeness. Laughter causes physical
reactions which stimulates the entire
somatic and neurological systems into
a more balanced symmetry. Moreover,
the muscular system gets a work out.
Did you ever guffaw until you fell? Your
muscular system completely relaxes,
You may lose your urine or even expel
gas-very unwillingly, but you cannot
stop roaring. Your circulatory system is
stimulated. Notice how red your face
becomes. Your respiratory system gets
a total workout as you inhale and
exhale deeply. The neurotransmitters
(i.e. probably the beta endorphin
hormones in the brain which signal
happiness) are working overtime. Such
good feelings are associated with the
person who stimulate a joyful response,
therefore creating a bond between the
couple.

Thus far in this book humor has been utilized to develop awareness and identify situations. Exaggeration is one aspect of comedy that distorts reality just enough to aid us to view ourselves in different perspectives that create more objective concepts.

The title, HOW TO TRAIN OUR HUSBAND TO BECOME AN ADULT, is a deliberate distortion of some basic truths that will-hopefully-crate a new demonstrable existence for women.

Irony, incongruous expectations of happenstance's that belie the expected outcome is another satirical method used, especially in Chapter 15, the repetitious aspects of daily housekeeping and baby tending represents the societal denial of women's work force contribution because it has no financial substance.

Work should be defined as: a responsibility which must be consistently accomplished for a major amount of hours per week in order that

mental/physical health, education, and/
or finances fulfills the survival needs of
life. After the World War researchers
discovered that children who are not
touched, except for feeding and
changing diapers, die! (see Spitz.a
Rene, bibliography). Therefore, the
loving hugs, games, and discipline that
is willingly given is nonetheless the
most necessary part of the
developmental stages of childhood
which requires tremendous amounts of
time and patience from the care giver. it
is work, but, somehow it is only defined
as such when we pay a nanny or baby
sitter. Ironic isn't it?

(Just as unloved children die, the self-
esteem of women die when their
contributions are denied. Women feel
as though they are the invisible half,
who only materializes when needed,
but ignored when she is needy).

The protestant work ethic which
stipulates: only if you work are you
good in the eyes of God: took on
another dimension in America when the

founding participants almost always became wealthy from hard work. Therefore hard work brought income and income and hard work melded into the personification of godliness. Since one was synonymous with the other, how could a woman be working because she never generates an income? Therefore woman must be cognizant of the cultural dictates that subliminally direct one half of the population to ignore the other half.

Initially, the Traditional gender-roles were not shaped for that purpose. In time, the obligations became a rigid obligation, not based on balanced work details as they were in the past, but instead fractured into multiple categories of mix and match roles from the resulting addition of other marital role models (i.e. Companionship and Partnership roles.) The categories offered in the latter chapter labelled, Role Rolls are, but a few of probably millions of different life style combinations which people fashion from the three differing role patterns. The reader is left to determine which combination of roles the bride and groom have gleaned as their own. A word of caution: the likelihood is that they have excerpted opposing role-rules for their own benefit, which then often creates conflicts.

For example: One of the Traditional Role duties of the couple is to reproduce with the male as the authority as to when and how frequency. This directive is totally opposite of the Equal Rights Role which allows a consensus between the two for lovemaking. Nor does its result have to have the motive of pregnancy, unless that is also their agreed upon goal.

Consequently, a male spouse that feels authorized to be in charge and adheres to the Traditional roles to produce children-at will-who is married to a female spouse who utilizes the Partnership Roles and uses sex for recreation purposes will have major conflicts between them until they determine the differing obligations and belief systems that are operating to tear them apart.

The resulting range of combinations of mismatched obligations can be huge.

Another example of the Traditional role is limiting the activities of the female as defined by the male, while he defines his as freedom to come and go as he determine.

The Partnership roles would be handled as an agreement made between the two determined by the couple's needs.

Hence couples need significant objectivity-if the marriage is to survive. The more objective a woman can be, the more able she is to utilize a comic approach in order to enlighten and direct her life toward happiness.

Developing the ability to deflect conflicts with Humor by identifying unlike situations with uniquely absurd, but understandable antidotes is another method to cement successful relationship[ps. In Chapter 14 Laura created a unlike situation with parallel characteristics to illustrate to Bob what he was unwilling to accept; which was that unusual circumstances need to be discussed to clear the misunderstandings and the consequential hurts of life.

Another type of absurdity; comparing contrasting viewpoints which was presented in the Frog fairy tales which sugar coated primary truths such as: we can only control ourselves, not others.

In Chapter 10, Tak bantered in order to illuminate hidden issues, to de-escalate anger, to divert an argument into pleasantries, to identify issues, and to create a close family ambience. Mal kept trying to divert authority back to him.

How is it that males can change the rules, make the rules, and then not abide by their own rules? How did men obtain this entitlement?

Men's rights is the major issue that most women wish to revolt against. However a women's revolutions is best won with hilarious overtures. Men's introduction to entitlements begin with his parents first words "It's a BOY!"

The Traditional role skews the perspective of parent, resulting in the little boy's behavior, which cause women to complain that men indulge themselves. In order to solve a problem, one must

understand the history of the issue. Therefore, the following information explores the intergenerational backgrounds that maintain the cultural axioms.

CHAPTER 17

IT'S A BOY

(Do frogs care what sex is born?)

This Chapter discusses male entitlements.

Although most of this material has been reviewed before in other writings, it's necessary to peruse it again in light of this material and also for those who somehow have not assimilated this information as yet. All of the following behaviors create the traits that the outdated Traditional Roles demand for marriage.

Mr. P.'s first child was a male. He triumphantly bellowed, "It's a Boy!"

Mr. R. announced, with a mellow smile, his first arrival "It's a girl."

And so begins the first imperceptible, entitlement, male, cultural, difference that is enacted by the attitudinal reactions to the genders.

Mr. P. and Mr. R. anxiously await their son's ability to catch a ball, so that they can play with them. Many men are quite not sure what to do with their daughters who they perceive to be too delicate to handle. (Again this has changed in some families, but I am discussing the situations where it remains concretely the same as in the past.)

The second minuscule step is set into motion; Traditional role concepts that dictate the male should be the aggressor, the female should be gentle and retiring.

For example:

Mrs. P. and Mrs. R. are friends. They are keeping their daughters entertained by letting them help make cookies. Their sons are outside rough housing. The boys come in, and request to cook beside their sister's. Mrs. P. and Mrs. R. exchange perplexed glances. "Why do you want to bake?" The boys pick up the unspoken taboo that's it's women's work which is stated in the body language and facial expressions of their mothers. The boys, then trade shrugs and with a bit of confusion. They say, "We really didn't want to." and run out to play again. The mothers feel relieved.

Mrs. P.'s son Peter is crying because Mrs. R.'s son has bashed him with a toy. A fist fight breaks out. The mothers ignore it with the comment to each other, "Boys will be boys." This is a perfect invitation to allow aggressive male behavior to fester. When he's grown, the wife is shoved, pushed, or worse, because he's been allowed to use physical force instead of negotiation to express his emotions.

Now the daughters are pushing each other. Both mothers state, "It's not lady like to brawl." They interest them in a puzzle. Soon all is quiet. Patience and yielding behavior is being modeled for the feminine traits of the Traditional Role.

Patricia, Mrs. P.'s girl is always climbing, gracefully swinging from the outside banister. Mrs. P. tells Pat to get down because she will fall. Pat falls and skins her knee. She cries. Both parents rush to pick her up, and comfort her, "My little Tom boy, where are you hurting?" Notice that her behavior is labelled masculine but, the treatment she receives is nurturing.

However, when clumsy Peter skins his leg, Mr. P.. says, "It's Al right. To Mrs. P. the father says, "Stop worrying, Mother!" Then Dad gruffly tells Peter, "Put some peroxide on it, and go out and play. You'll be fine." Peter howls. No one pays attention.

Peter is experiencing the social taboos that boys must take risks, be aggressive, and take pain without showing emotion. (These comprise the Traditional traits that can be traced to biblical times when the male was the total authority in the household over time, resources, place to live and even life or death.) The next time Peter will ignore his discomfort. Since his pain is diminished, he diminishes the pain of others. In time, he will neither be aware of his own emotions or that of others. As an adult, his wife wants him to acknowledge her hurt feelings. He doesn't relate to them. He's unable to respond.

Peter has begun a process of segmenting his personality. His normal responses are buried. Objective logic, based on Traditional concepts, is encouraged. He observes the difference in the manner in which he, as well as all his boyhood friends are treated, and he concludes he's better/ stronger than his sister and all other females because he has mastered the art of detachment. This is the first lesson in differentiating genders according to the cultural precepts. Take the logic one step further, males are programmed for struggle (i.e., competitive living). Businesses have preferred, and still do prefer a single-minded impersonal focus on affairs.

Women tend to be concerned (the nurturing trait) about how they feel, how their co-workers feel, what is fair, and so forth. If females reacts to an injustice or a disturbance, the boss remarks, "It's that time of the month again?" Women who join the work force: either alter their work responses to comply with the rationale or are limited in their access toward climbing the corporate ladder.

However, an underlying weakness is developing within the male's personality. Anyone who is not allowed to vent their anguish, buries it with ghosts of inconsistencies which might take the form of using foul language, or violence towards their wives. Only understanding our culture, and healing the wounds will the recurrent deviant behaviors be eliminated.

Here is a metaphor to illustrate the healing process; Marsha, a two hundred multiple personality seen on the Spring 1991 TV's Sixty Minutes, whose torturous childhood was aided by encouraging her inner child to externalize the abuse, which allowed her to begin to heal her wounds.

The boy is emotionally wounded from the abandonment he feels when he's not nurtured when he hurts. The abuse, of not allowing him to vent in a socially acceptable peaceful manner, is not recognized as abuse. It is considered, instead, as shaping the male for his role in society.

Also note the female counterpart is one-half of a healthy personality. Patricia is allowed to cry. She is fussed over when she is hurt. Her subliminal message is that as a female she will be protected and will pattern her behavior from the nurturing she has received.

This split is important to note in both the male and female. There are many more that will be examined, but this first splinter begins the education of both sexes to accept Traditional roles.

Even though the male is taught conscientiousness in order to be the sole family supporter, he lacks dependability for family endeavors which he considers to be the feminine responsibility,

(i.e. Sending his own Mother a Mother's Day card is left for is wife to do.) Moreover, the Traditional role has put blinders on a man to believe himself to be the main provider. Yet, the majority of women are working today. Many have competitive salaries. How about that! It isn't necessary to batter the male's image of himself to toughen him, for what? He now has help supporting the family. Especially after marriage, the women expects and values a sensitive man who can comprehend and respond to his own and her emotional needs. Lack of a skilled listening response creates undue stress.

Today's war is with stress! It kills more of us through depleting the immune system so that we can't fight the viruses and bacteria which invade us daily. Now scientists are even aware that cancer, and arthritis and other illnesses are stress related. All of the evolving roles create stress.

Moreover, there is a constant reinforcement to maintain a Traditional tough image. "Cry baby. Cry baby." his peers call him as the tears run down his cheeks. He'll make every effort, and succeed, to not show that display again.

The Traditional role is tenacious. It prevents creative thinking. A male client of mine was amazed when I taught him communication skills exactly like those he had already learned on the job. "Do you mean, all I have to do is apply, what I already do at work, at home, and I'll solve my problems? I never thought of it," he said.

Married women want men to be mature. In order to be mature one must have the capacity to understand one's actions in the context of the situation, and to accept the consequences of their behaviors. Moreover, the individual must accept the responsibility for participating in the efforts of marriage.

The following are typical examples which illustrate the males responses to women's work needs:

Example: 1.

With the advent of suburb living, the husband has expanded the duties of the wife. Therefore the rusting iron railing, the house needing painting, the gardening all become a woman's job. The wife states, "When are you going to put putty around those windows?" The husband says,

"Oh, 'I'll get to it. I promise." Ten years later the house is in severe disrepair. The wife paints the house. The husband arrives home, and says, "Why didn't you let me do that?"

2. Mom asks Dad to help her. Dad says to the daughter, "Marianne dry the dishes." Mom says, I wanted you to accept your share of the responsibility, not ask our daughter to do it." Dad

says, "What are you complaining about? The dishes got dried didn't they?"

A twelve year old boy refuses to do the dishes because that's woman's work. He's ashamed and embarrassed if forced to comply. In 2000 years the grade schools and high schools peer groups still reflect an 1880's gender mentality. A teacher/client recently agreed with that remark and said, "But, it is becoming more brutal, the teenage boys call the girls, "Bitches and Cunts!" In fact, I surveyed a number of teachers from the L.I. area. All the high school teachers agreed that the Traditional role is still functioning and being accepted by both sexes.

3. A mother of a fifteen year old male explains that she puts in a forty hour week of work, plus cooking, cleaning, laundry, and running him to his football practice, and therefore requests him to pickup his room. His response is, "That's a mother's job." She says, "I'm

not your slave. Clean up your room."
He says, "Well I won't be your slave,
either."

There is not the capacity to understand
a flexible situation because the
Traditional Roles dictate roles to
perform specific tasks as if we were
performing a part in a Stage Play. The
son is pointing out that mother is not
following the script. It is easier for him
to identify with the male's role and
therefore comply, if he's asked to mow
the lawn. Moreover he has noted that
Dad treats Mom as a slave, in that, the
father doesn't contribute to lessening
the workload; therefore, slavery is the
condition of the Traditional role. Since
housework is not his duty, he feels
demoralized if he assumes it.

A conversation took place between a
husband and his wife. He told her, he
only did what he wanted to do (i.e. only
his job). Employed also, she was
amazed to find that when she mirrored
her husband's attitude of accepting only
obligations that she wanted to do, she

no longer remember—ed to do the laundry. Her husband complained that he hadn't clean clothes, to which she responded that she would run the washing machine as soon as she needed outfits, but as yet she hadn't run out. He took over the laundry duties because he wanted his things done weekly. The point to this story is that the male had refused to help do feminine chores, until he finally recognized a need to accomplish them. What's more it was the wife's first cognizance of the male's perspective that something that she had completed weekly for years was overlooked by her, now, merely by the assumption that it wasn't her responsibility anymore. By using this

new insight the wife was able to motivate him to assume responsibility with the household chores.

Therefore a few of the basic tenets of developing responsibility were partially met. Lets review how to develop reliable behavior, whether for child rearing or husband training:

The ability to comprehend dependable behavior within the context of varying circumstances. (The changing marital obligations are beyond many male's ken because they are not primarily effected. The secondary reaction stemming from the wife's anger is met with confusion and or misapprehension. A need for an understanding of the consequences of inaction. (The divorced male can't relate to where he failed.)

One needs to leave a vacuum that an individual can fill voluntarily. (Women need to let the work go undone, so that the male can replace her activities with his sweat.)

All individuals need to contribute something noteworthy in their lives, (but is housework considered noteworthy by anyone?).

Perhaps we need to pause here, before we go on with the process of building maturity. The above examples return us to the Traditional role concept that housewives don't work.

Note this illustration:

The husband says: "That's not work. Where's your pay check? " As the husband repairs their car, the wife says: "That's not work. Why are you fusing? No one is paying you." The husband says, "Of course I'm working. This is difficult to do." His wife counters with, "How the story changes when you're the one doing the unpaid labor."

The repetitious nature of the work is negated when a male scrubs the floor once with his wife keeping the children at bay. He decides the task simple. It never occurs to him that she must oversee the children and mop the floor at the same time, or the work would never be done. It never occurs to him until he is divorced or widowed, and then he is overwhelmed. However, the demoralization of housework developed in a more subliminal manner than that.

This premise is worth reiterating:

Housework is unpaid labour. No one works for nothing, so women are not working. The Protestant work ethic states that work is equivalent to godliness. Almost any type of employment, except keeping one's own house in order, brought Americans the riches they left their countries to accomplish. Money, and work became inseparable in the U.S.A. psyche, as the reward for work. No salary, no labour; but work the American woman does do. Outside employment, as well as household and child-care duties create the modern slave. Her children recognize this attitude and frequently treat her as such. She often has difficulty making them mind. Then those children grow-up, the boys become husbands who ignore the slaves' (i.e., their wives') opinions, feelings, and needs. Moreover, the male blames the outbursts of frustration on PMS. This keeps the woman off-balance, for everything she feels is blamed on being a woman. Her logic is considered unstable and thus unworthy of consideration.

Women need to understand the dynamics of the total situation before they can combat the problem within their own home. Women must be aware that maturity is a goal for every individual in order to develop a sense of belonging and of identity. Today's housewife is left with a hollow, loneliness because she has been stripped of dignity. (Society defines it as: housewife blues). Her outlet is a recognized career that returns her sense of self-worth. No wonder, our sons and our husbands want nothing to do with housework! Who wants to work for minus a pay check, and minus self esteem.

Another example:

There was a man who did the laundry without being asked. After carrying it upstairs, he complained that his back hurt. His wife retorted: "If it's not work, how can your back hurt?"

Resources such as money allows control over ones environment. Again the housework is unrewarding. Did you ever see an advertisement that read?:

A CAREER TOO GOOD TO MISS!

Housewife occupation!

THERE IS NO GUARANTEE FOR ANY OF THE BELOW ITEMS:

No vacations

No medical insurance

No sick time. Work right through illness.

No salary!

No advancement ever!

We will never praise you. We promise to look over your shoulder and criticize everything you do. After an indefinite period of time you may be let go without advance notice for a worker with apparently more likable qualities.

How can anyone pass up such a valuable opportunity!! Advertising for slave household opportunities can be very challenging. Try presenting this advertisement to your sluggish husband the next time you'd like him to assist you.

Seriously though, what significance does organization and cleanliness abilities have if it's non-existentially viewed? Do men wait in line to offer their services for housework that is not their choice and is pressed on them? Why should they do that, when they have women ready and willing to be their servants? Especially when men believe that they are fulfilling the exact requirements of the predetermined Traditional script.

Instead the outside employed woman performs the good mother, good wife role that compliments the macho ideas of servitude. She spoils the male by doing everything for him rather than weather the storm of confrontation to require an assessment for balancing the workload. Why not go on strike?

Hand him a contract that stipulates your terms:

NEW CONTRACTUAL TERMS

Work to be halved by both spouses. Work related duties are defined as: cooking supper, doing laundry, scrubbing floors/walls/windows, food shopping, diapering/bathing and watching the kids, playing and reading to them, as well as secretarial and accounting duties, plus gardening, and all types of repairs.

Salary: An exchange of thank yous, hugs, and kisses.

Note that one must be explicit. Don't assume that any member of your household knows what is expected. Recount the details of what you want.

Labor mutually executed, should also be mutually appreciated by both parties with one another. Break the Traditional attitudinal hold on your life. Isn't there another saying? Cleanliness is Godliness. God made an orderly world in seven days. If men don't want to share women's overload, let them become God. He did the work all alone.

I am including an article I wrote about gender differences that is applicable to this Chapter.

8/24/09 Male Gender Differences by Bernadine Fawcett:

As far back as literature is known to go, men have been trying to figure out women. Volumes have been written about the mystic of womanhood. In 1995, Yale brain researchers, Bennett Shaywitz and Sally Shaywitz, asked nonsensical questions of both men and women while they electronically monitored the brain activity. The biological differences in each became evident; which prepares the genders for different interpretations creating minuscule and major misunderstandings. The males' left hemisphere lit up while the female used both left and right hemispheres to process language. Men hear things logically with their left part of the cerebrum, while women use both areas which includes the right part which is the emotional/creative area.

Since men misunderstand women's reactions, the majority of men withdraw or become angry when confronted with female emotions. The silent treatment sends most females up the wall because they interpret the reaction as lack of caring and loss of love.

A large portion of the clients that I see have these gender difficulties. The husband or lover believes that the woman needs help handling her life when she is only venting about her issues. A Lover needs to listen to what emotions the wife is expressing and let her know he "gets it" . He needs to verbally detail her frustrations, abandonment, hurt, etc. until she feels a sense of relief that he knows her depth. Unfortunately this exercise is not handled well as many men have spent their entire life not dealing with deep affections and instead substitute sexual sensations for the essence of life.

Women, also, are confused by the male response after marriage . It seems cold, indifferent and unloving. During courtship males have oxytocin which is constantly predominant in females. It is responsible for her deeper affective behavior. When oxytocin biologically disappears in men after a commitment, the women feel abandoned. Women, also need to learn to be more specific with their needs, wants and desires. I, often feel like tearing my hair out, when a women says that she does not want to hurt the man's feelings by being direct. Whereas, the man tells me he does not know what his partner wants. Many a man breathes a sigh of relief in my office when the counterpart is explicit. Now he knows what to do.

Women become extremely frustrated when they do give clear specific messages only to have the men ignore or misinterpret. them. Professional counseling will aide that problem.

Learning to listen from the opposite point of view is a skill best learned in counseling. Once learned the sexes can co-ordinate their daily life and the love life that had become damaged from the misunderstandings which resulted from dissimilar definitions from a seemingly identical vocabulary. Once the definitions are on a level plane the relationship can stabilize.

Is it possible to disconnect all the Traditional dictums and create egalitarianism? Perhaps Chapter 18, will answer that question.

The next Chapter "Roles Rolls" exemplifies most of the roles and the role splintering that has happened as a result of the cultural revolution.

CHAPTER 18

ROLES ROLLS

(What a froggy idea!)

There are three major marital roles which splinter into an additional three, but in actuality there are nearly as many variations as the population because of the result of the ethnic diversity within this culture and the manner in which couples create their own lifestyles to best suit their own lifestyle.

THE CONFUSION OF ROLES

Picture Mr. X. sprawled across the bed with his feet and legs spread just like his name in a X. His wife is perched on a five inch sliver of the bed. She said, "Honey, I'm nearly off the bed, move over." He sleepily fully outstretches his arm, "I'm practically off the bed now!" he said. With that, he rolls towards her and embraces her. She is pushed off her precarious perch by a groggy husband leaving the vacancy which is snatched up by her slumbering husband. She sleeps on the couch that night.

How many wives spend most of their married lives on the couch because it's the only place to sleep?

Mr. X. doesn't feel obliged to learn how to share his bed. As a child, he slept alone. As an adult, he is sleeping alone, also. However, he isn't aware of it because his wife sneaks back in bed with him about an hour before he awakens.

However, Mr. X. awoke one night around midnight, searched for his wife, found her on the couch, and bellowed, "My wife beds with me, not the couch!" His wife said,, "Why are you jealous of the couch?"

Mr. X. exhibited the decision making and authoritarian aspects of what he believes to be his rights as dictated by the Traditional role model. God told

Abraham to sacrifice his only begotten son as proof that he followed God's dictates. That is a powerful life/death sentence of male authority. (God is envisioned as a male. He begins the male-lineage of control.) The majority of countries that have a Judaeo-Christian heritage expose the Traditional role. This role obfuscates the mature roles of equally shared responsibilities. No one changes unless they are directly hurt by circumstances. Mr. X. enjoyed full access to the mattress, so why should he change?

The Mrs. does not benefit by the Traditional roles, therefore, her retort reflects her decision to be free to select her own bedding arrangements. After a initial trepidation she chooses the Partnership roles.

You thought the main point was over who should sleep in the bed all night? The real issue is whether the wife should follow the Traditional Role that allows her husband to be lord and master or whether they have an equal right to decisions according to the Partner Role concepts.

The significance of who governs can become ludicrous, as illustrated by Mr. C. who had been unemployed for five years. His wife, earned whatever small income, as a secretary as she could. Her years of financial sacrifice for her husband and children had depleted her business wardrobe.

Mr. C. demanded that Mrs. C. return the suit she purchased.

Mrs. C: I bought you a suit, last year, which you haven't worn yet.

Mr. C.: If you get one. I get one. That's fair.

Mrs. C : How many suits do you think you need? Tell me and I'll purchase them for you. Now that I think of it you owe me one. I didn't purchase one when I bought yours. How is it you didn't remind me how unfair that was? The point is the suit is needed in order to maintain my employment. You are not working. If you needed a suit for work, you would have to purchase it.

Everyone with children will have recognized, "But you got one for Susie. Where is mine?" Immaturity is again disguised as the male Traditional entitlements to determine the family purchases. Mrs. C states her boundaries and demands equality.

Most of today's problems are the mismatching of role responsibilities and corresponding obligations that each partner expects of the other. A large segment of Traditionally oriented males establish the right to have first say, only say, and a skewed say in all matters. This puts males on the unthinking, demanding levels, of an infant. Baby wakes up and screams for food. Baby does not consider that mommy is exhausted. The inability or refusal to understand another point of view relegates the male to the infant level.

Examples of Traditional male spurious entitlements

Flirtatious John may be asserting teenage rebellion when he dailies with other women. He is demonstrating his right to show-off. His wife, Alice positions herself directly opposite him between her women friends. She loudly laughs, "If you think he's charming now, you should see him when he comes home from a hard-day's work." At that moment, John would love to rub a genie bottle and make a wish to have Alice disappear.

John relegates Alice to his fantasy of wish fulfillment: an object of desire, to fulfill John's adolescent wishes of who, when, where, and the amount that he wants sexually. This type of thinking disallows his wife's intelligence. It is another Traditional caveat.

She becomes in his eyes an object which does not command very much attention.

Alice has used put-down satire that will backlash on her. However, she probably doesn't want her marriage anymore anyway, due to her spouses disloyalty.

Another Example:

Mr. W. walks in the door, gives his wife a distracted kiss, opens a beer, flicks on the TV, and then settles down to the perfect life.

Mrs. W. waits for the commercial to inform him of the day's events. "I mailed the package you wanted sent. The kids got their report cards today. Andrew got an A. Julia got a D in Math." Mrs. W. suspects that her husband hasn't heard a word she said. She continues, "The roof was torn off by a tornado. Today, Julia started her first day of prostitution. Andrew jumped off the Empire State building. He thought he could fly." Then she screamed, "You're not listening to a word I said!"

Mr. W. looks towards her and says, "Yes I did. I heard every word. You said. The kids started some new projects and there are flies in the house. We really must get an exterminator."

Who listens to the ramblings of a housewife? The Traditional role, as interpreted today, encourages unrestricted thoughtlessness. The teenager doesn't call home because the youth knows where s/he is. The Traditional role takes on the narcissistic attitudes of youth. Nor does the career/ partnership fare any better. Mrs. A. suggests a new logo for their family floral business; Letters shaped to look like flowers. Her spouse flatly turned the idea down. Three months latter, Mr. A. announces his original concept: A logo with letters in the form of a flower.

Both housewives and career women agendas should include equality with their husbands. (This is America. Right?) However the Traditional role tenuously prevents men from acknowledging that a female could possibly have anything to discuss that would interest them. Sometimes the the career women's income and skills may even surpass those of her husband's, making her-at least his equal financially.

However, his Traditional conditioning that he maintains the alpha role placing her condescendingly beneath him. Again the mismatching of the expectations of the Partnership roles and the Traditional roles creates instead an infantile male role.

For Example:

Mrs. A. said, "Do you want to join me at the Boston Business Convention next Friday?"

Mr. A. said, "Ah huh."

Mrs. A. said, "Good! I'll make reservations."

Mr. A. arrived home to find his suitcase packed and his wife was ready to leave.

He said, "Why are you leaving me? You're even taking my suitcase!" A teenager processes information in the same manner. They live in their own world. Inform a teenager that the family is traveling to Niagara Falls on vacation, and the information will be twisted to mean that s/he can stay at a friend's house during the same time period.

Distorted Traditional Roles again allow the male to determine, his rights as a male which he interprets to mean the right to be disrespectful. After being interrupted for an hour by Jack, Jane's finished her story in this manner:

Jane: Last Wednesday we-

Jack: It was Tuesday, not Wednesday.

Jane: Last Tuesday I dug a ditch.

Jack: How could you have done that? Where is it?

Jane: (lightly quipping) You'll find yourself in it, if you interrupt me again.

Jane's ten-year-old interrupts her telephone conversations continually. Husband should not demand attention when his wife is on the phone He should act his age, not his daughter's age.

Jane anticipates the cooperation of Partnership roles which allows both spouses equal responsibilities and obligations for the relationship, for romance, for financial obligations, for career efforts, for child-care, and for maintaining the household duties.

However, if men don't assume their equal share the women feel cheated, and often feel guilty that somehow they failed. The only failure was; to assume that men haven't realized that a sexual revolution for equal rights is raging under their noses. Neither gender realizes the cultural devastation of changing roles. Men follow the Traditional roles, but follow the Partnership roles when it's to their advantage. (Women mismatch also and with the same dysfunctional result). This one-sided unreasoning logic again locates people on the adolescent level of right and wrong.

Husbands who expect their wives to tell them what has to be accomplished, are hiding behind the Traditional role that justifies such a comments as: "You only have to tell what has to be done, and I'll help you." That is equivalent to what kids say: Well you didn't tell me you wanted the dishes washed.

Sharing the Partnership load is accepting the responsibility of organizing and accomplishing work. Traditionally men have not been taught to sort clothes and run a dishwasher. Men who are mechanically inclined have been known to state: "I don't know how to run the washer." The excuse is not entirely pleading ignorance as much as it is a disassociation of self. The macho image separates the male into a one-half of a person. Just as a woman who accepts the traits of being dependent, yielding and submissive is the other half. We need compete personalities to compete in today's world.

When I was a kid I watched my father and then later I watched my husband repair cars. I even helped. However, I could never identify a problem or repair a car. Just as men have watched their mother's and sometimes their wives prepare food, they couldn't prepare a meal. Neither gender felt it necessary to assimilate that information because the job held a gender status. (There are some changes now, but it is not across the board).

It stands to reason then that some males need to be taught; how to make a bed, how to sort the laundry, how to put a diaper on a child and so forth. Women were taught in home economics, and/or at their Mother's elbow. However, after showing him, if he still pleads ignorance, then the Traditional role has created blinders and resistance that stall him at the teenage level. After all, Teenagers use any excuse to get out of work.

Another role causes a mix and match dysfunction. It is the Companionship Role. The wife believes that along with all her other functions, she should be beautiful, intelligent, and charming. For example, Mrs. B. dolls up in an exquisite slinky dress for a social occasion. Her husband says, "Where the h--l do you think your going? I'm not going to have my wife ogled at." His wife says, "You have something, they can't get. Let their eyes fall out." The Traditional male role demands that the husband be protective and loyal towards his wife. The male says, "I'll gouge their eyes out if they look!" The male is as possessive as a two year old with a favorite toy which is not shared, even for a moment. However, his mate refuses the authoritarian stance and adheres to the Companionship role obligations by maintaining her beauty and her right to dress as she chooses.

Mrs. B. expects Mr. B. to romantically give her presents. He feels the same glee as his children as he opens his gifts. He believes he has done his share by giving her. money so that she can select the gift she wants. The following year, she reciprocates with a gift of money which she earned from her part-time job. He is disappointed. Money is not very exciting. So, he converts from the Traditional role of showing only loyalty: to the Companionship role to match his wife's romantic responses.

The three major marital roles mentioned in the text are:

1. TRADITIONAL

2. COMPANIONSHIP

3. EQUAL OR PARTNERSHIP

These roles were originally predominant in our society as separates categories. The previous depictions have illustrated the mismatching of the three roles. From these three types, there are diversified offshoots. In the defense of men, many women are as confused by the mix and match combinations. Assorted outfits, as women well know, must be put together with some type of guidelines or the ensemble is outlandish. Turn the hodgepodge analogy into marital role disorganization, and we have outrageous conflicts arising from the dissenting attitudes that determine the nuptial obligations. The problem is that no one can outline the lifestyle of the couple. It is the result of each individual's family of origin. (Our heritage stems from the multiple ethnic groups who mainly endorsed the Traditional roles, but each group had unique interpretations of them. Now intermarriage for generations has created a melting pot that is not as identical in practice as it is in concept. (For example, the Spanish nobility allowed clandestine affairs for men, but women hadn't the same privilege). Neither knows what the other perceives as his or her obligation. Therefore, the analogy of mix-matched clothes becomes invisible, but definitely there. Imagine putting on a suit of clothes, but your partner thinks you are naked. Neither partner responds to the clothes (Roles) of the other because neither perceives them.

But first a historical perspective of the three marital roles must be presented here, in order to reduce the confusion caused by couples who unwittingly combine fragments of the original three functions. (Traditional, Companionship, Partnership)

1. THE TRADITIONAL ROLE

The traditional role has a definitive script to follow, much as actors in a play, the spouses must keep their lines straight. The women had been refined to be nurturing, dependent, submissive, gullible, gentle, unobtrusive, cautious, compassionate, and love children. I was amazed to find a pamphlet, amongst my mother-in-law's things, that was published in the eighteen-hundred's by the U.S. Government that depicted ladies behavior as never saying 'No". She was born in that century and had passive resistance down to a science. She would say, "What restaurant would you like to go to?" If we suggested one which she did not choose, then she would say, "Wouldn't you rather go to Friendly's or Captain Bill's?" If we dissented she would give us other choices, refraining from mentioning our selection. This routine could go on for hours. As long as we disagreed with her, she would keep suggesting a selection until there was an agreement or we were worn into submission. It was frustrating. Unfortunately I never found the information until after she died.

Then another author and psychologist of that era, Stanley Granville Hall wrote professional books indoctrinating the proper college atmosphere for the frailer and more vulnerable sex who needed protection. There was no doubt about the depictions of a women's role. It was clear and restrictive. Women were meant to be housewives and mothers with limited domestic authority.

Our society was composed of immigrants from across the waters who brought the Traditional role traits with them, creating a gender culture that cut people's personalities into halves. One half of the personality was called woman and the other half of the personality was called man. Women were weaned to be the subjective part, and men were trained to handle the objective half. This resulted in a split personality for both which never made a whole even from the times from which it sprung. In the eighteen-hundreds Freud treated the resulting paralysis as hysteria, because women had no choice other than domesticity (unless you include prostitution as a choice). Very few women fled to the free life of Greenwich Village. That Bohemian outcast lifestyle was not an option for the proper women. Her immobility signified her emotional state of entrapment.

Moreover, men were brought up to be leaders, able to take risks, be dominant, independent, individualistic, decisive, self-reliant, competitive, assertive, aggressive, analytical and most importantly have rights and take emotional and/or physical blows without breaking down. Boys had their own belief system internalized in gangs, or clubs. Masculine traits prepared men for war, for careers, and for the Traditional role in marriage. Men dealt logically and objectively with life. What men were not prepared for was how to deal with relationships.

Relationships and the communication required, no matter how circumventive, was the only thing that women were allowed to do. The wife's life was totally submissive. The Traditional duties prepared the wife to rear her children, keep a nice home, while she accepted a subordinate position economically and socially plus accepting the male's determination of residence. Females accepted the limitations imposed on their activities, leisure time, and choice of friends. The extended family took-over most of her free-time. The main purpose of intercourse was dutifully imposed to insure propagation of the kinship line. One senior citizen in an old-age home irately told me that she was delighted that sex-business was finally over!

Since the male Traditional part allowed the husband the right to determine the time and amount of sex, without the consent of his wife; no wonder the aged-lady was relieved she no longer had

to perform this duty. It was never her pleasure. All the male obligations that bolster the Traditional function were developed for an authoritarian atmosphere that did little to improve a loving relationship. Only if the wife were un-rebelliously submissive to the husband's decisions, in every aspect of their-lives, could there be a willing bondage. Men kept their leisure and work time separate from their wives. Men were expected to be loyal, grateful, and respectful of their wives. Most men were respectful, but often not loyal. Women ignored men dallying because the divorce option was not an option for a lady. It put her on the level of a tramp. The wife's devotion was rewarded with economic security and protection.

The Traditional male of that time would have said and even some of the men of our time do say:

"I expect my wife to be there when I want her. She really needs my protection. She could get assaulted or raped if she's out at nightfall. It's not necessary for her to work. I provide everything she'll ever need. I'll work two jobs if need be. She visits with her women friends or relatives when I have my business associates over for dinner. I am the master and owner of my castle. The perfect wife is the one who never needs to be told to stay in line. I appreciate all she does within the home."

The Traditional female of yesteryear (luckily there are not too many submissive women left) would have said: "I'll live wherever my husband has to work. He's the one that supports us. He has the last word on disciplining the children. I'm often not sure how to handle things. I prefer to defer to my husband's decisions in all major matters. I'd never admit it to another soul, but I'd prefer not to have that dirty sex thing. Maybe he'll find a mistress as my friend's husband has. After all there are only so many times you can have a headache.

2 . THE COMPANIONSHIP ROLE

In the Companionship role, the woman's role is subordinate only to the male's occupation. She accepted the lifestyle when she agreed to marry him. It's a strange way to choose your employment, second-hand. Yet, once the choice is determined by the marriage vows, the wife must be supportive, emotionally/intellectually, and maintain and sustain a charming demeanor that will enhance his career. The husband must economically, chivalrously, and romantically sustain his wife's efforts. He must provide funding to support her attire, her recreational/educational/social, and leisure activities in order that his pursuits be complimented by his wife's contributions. The Companionship role is an extension of the male-self-hood. However, there is seldom much conflict with this application, even though it prevents a woman from developing her own career. It is a positive cultural self-image that women are encouraged to maintain. Therefore she derives her sense of self from performing according to the current social demands. The inspirational part of her is curtailed, but in most cases she is rewarded sufficiently with praise and improved financial and social status that most women seldom feel a loss of self esteem. In fact, in most cases there is no loss, because she can fashion what she does in creative ways to express herself.

The male says: I love her dearly. I need her to make a good impression upon my constituents/customers/associates.

The female says: I gladly accede to his career. I enjoy dressing beautifully, maintaining my figure, and keeping abreast of the times. It is stimulating even though my motivation and raison d'être emanates from him.

In my practice I have found that there are exceptions to the satisfaction with this role. In the event that a woman held a different view point of her life either from the beginning or having it switched on her because of the need for business networking.

The other exception is when the Traditional housewife is expected to perform both duties of both roles without the monetary support. Even more importantly she hasn't the time to engage in the additional beauty, education and so forth that supports the Companionship role. Since many American women aspire to improving themselves, this creates another conflict for which she frequently assumes full blame.

3. THE PARTNERSHIP OR EQUAL ROLES

The Classic Partnership obligations are equal in every aspect. The male takes over whatever work is undone, just as his mate does for him. This is a partnership in every respect. Both spouses participate economically according to their earning ability.

There is no separation of roles. Male designated jobs such as snow blowing, mowing the lawn, mechanical and electrical jobs are negotiated according to the experience, aptitude and strength, of the individual not according to sex differences. So called female duties of diapering, shopping, cooking are accomplished by whomever is available at the time.

Love making, is a shared-caring which takes place, when there is mutual acquiescence.

The husband says: I love holding my children. I feel sorry for my Dad. He missed this! No one enjoys changing a poo-py diaper, but it has to be done. My wife and I are professional people. We check our schedules whenever our schedules might conflict with the normal routine in order that we might make baby sitting arrangements, if they're necessary. As a family we are very active together. The children look forward to the company of other children at nursery school. My wife is a better electrician and is more mechanical than I, but I can hold my own in those fields also. We both take on do it yourself projects. What we don't know or can't do-we hire someone, which is no reflection on any of us.

I guess I would say that open and constant communication is the glue that unifies our marriage. We both have the freedom to socialize and pursue activities that include both sexes. We trust each other to maintain our vows.

The wife says: I feel good about myself and our marriage. The children will be able to follow our role models into the next generation. My husband has spoken my thoughts about equal application. I don't need to add to them.

The egalitarian couple are mature people. They may misunderstand each other, but they are willing to discuss issues. If that doesn't resolve their conflict, they look for objective counseling. Each spouse may look to the other for comfort. In that case they switch from a child stance to a parental, in the most positive of reciprocal nurturing which does not overburden either spouse.

In other words, the Classic Partnership allows for either partner to occasionally act immaturely. Since both are there for each other. They discuss the behavior if it causes relationship-damage, or accept it if one person needs comforting.

Neither partner controls the other. There is no need to control or train each other. Both are adults. This is the model marriage that this book encourages. The title, HOW TO TRAIN YOU HUSBAND TO BECOME AN ADULT will delight- both sexes because the egalitarian male will laugh at whatever idiosyncrasies he has retained from a culture that dictated the Traditional role of macho not so long ago. He will be pleased to identify and eliminate whatever inconsistencies that would undermine his marriage. In fact, I'm delighted to report that in reading this manuscript to a writer's group one retired policeman roared with laughter at the title and said, "I want a copy of the book when it's published."

The mix-matching of the three roles developed male subcategories. The six mix-matches presented here are, but a minuscule suggestion of the multiple spinoffs that differing life styles have created. As you peruse the six categories, pick the one which best fits your husband's role choice. Then you will not only know how he is dressed (role), but also what suit of clothes (role choice) he has chosen (metaphorically speaking).

TYPES OF RELATIONSHIP ROLES The combined categories are:

THE DISTORTED '90'S TRADITIONAL ROLE

TRADITIONAL/PARTNERSHIP/
COMPANIONSHIP

THE BLINDED TRADITIONAL

THE CON-ARTIST TRADITIONAL

THE CONFUSED/BORDERLINE/
PARTNERSHIP/THE DEVIANT TRADITIONAL

THE DISTORTED '90's TRADITIONAL ROLE

In today's world the Traditional Role is a warped edition of the classic Traditional Role. The male who clings to the old roles feels betrayed by a wife whom he classifies under many unattractive names such as b----, c---, and so forth.

All the literature on equal rights has not penetrated his brain, and if it has, he has swept it aside as not pertaining to his situation. He thinks that his wife is happy, because he is happy. He's happy because he snaps his fingers and his wife jumps. After his wife leaves him, he wonders if her complaints had some validity? It has all the marks of a teenager's attitude that, it can't happen to me, and life is fun only if taken without contemplative plans.

Rigid is best defined in this context as a male who adheres to the ancient role. He won't budge one inch from his sole breadwinner role. He sees no inconsistencies in the fact that his wife is employed, yet he is still the controller of major economic and domestic decisions. He cannot and will not understand anything that is labelled feminine. After all as a child he was mocked when he fancied long hair and jewelry. He quickly forgot the scalding remarks, but subliminally incorporated them into anger projected towards females in his adult life. Therefore, he feels ashamed if his wife is employed since he believes he's inadequate because he's unable to support his family without her help. Should she work because she enjoys it, his hostility knows no boundaries for embarrassing him. Regardless of the work circumstances he refuses to raise even one little finger to help his wife. He adheres to the outdated Traditional model and believes that his wife should assume the corresponding obligations. Since his wife follows the equal rights concepts he believes she is undermining his male identity.

He says: How dare she be independent and assertive? I expect my wife to be home watching the children, with supper ready when I arrive home. Not gallivanting about with her friends. She has no right working. I'll take two jobs if necessary. She could get assaulted or raped if she's out past nightfall. I think it's sluttish for her to talk to the male co-workers under the parking lot spotlights. How dare she work? She only does it because she likes it. I'll put a stop to that. I'm master and owner of my castle. She'd better not get out of line. This tirade frequently manifests itself in the form of jealousy.

The immature male is hiding behind the skirts of Tradition and will not acknowledge any contribution from his wife as valid. This encompasses household duties expected of her, and therefore minimized, or outside employment negated because it doesn't conform to the the male's outlook. In fact, the husband believes that anything a woman does is easy, enjoyable, and non-exhaustive. He does not do housework. The male clings to Peter Pan fantasies because it serves his purpose. Then he need not acknowledge the overload his wife carries.

For example: Mrs. Z. was bending in an uncomfortable upside down position as she painted the wood awning over her head. Mr. Z. said, "You only do what you have fun doing." His wife then said, "Well I've had all the fun I can stand for today, so you take over now. I really wouldn't want to take away your pleasure."

The Traditional wife of today says:

I'm both his mother and his child. I'm not sure when he wants which. Just as my teenage son is maturing and expects me to know when he wants me to mother him and when he wants to be treated as an equal. I never know what curve my mate will send me next. My husband won't accept my opinions. He restricts the resources such as money, or the vehicle, if I do not comply with his demands. He gets angry because he expects me to do his business accounting. He won't allow me my choice of outside employment. Whatever he decrees is my work is then added to my load.

Regardless of how much appreciation the male shows, the Traditional traits foster dependent and co-dependent personalities for both genders. Characteristics of dependence, independence, supportiveness, assertiveness, cooperativeness, etc., model a well rounded personality. The updated Traditional role begins the lower end of the continuum which maximizes into aberrant behaviors which are discussed in more detail under THE DEVIANT TRADITIONAL.

THE TRADITIONAL/PARTNERSHIP/ COMPANIONSHIP

This type may be any combination of the three basic roles. For example, both partners share careers and finances symmetrically (Partnership role). The women is intelligent, capable, and attires herself elegantly (which are components of the Companionship role). However the wife is the major child-caregiver (Traditional role obligation).

The husband says:

We need two incomes to survive. I try to share the housework. I cook when I arrive home before she does. (Equal roles up to this point). I don't know a thing about children, that's her domain. (This is a cop out. Women have to learn as they raise children also. The male is hiding under the cloak of the Traditional role in order that he doesn't have to be bothered. Refusing responsibility for whatever reason places him in the adolescent stage.) I insist that my wife keep herself up. Our romantic life depends on it. (which is segment of the Companionship role).

The wife says:

I like to be attractive. It adds zest to my life. I feel better about myself. We budget and make all our decisions together. My major complaint is that he won't play with the kids. He ignores them as if they were non-existent.

THE BLINDED TRADITIONAL

The Blinded Traditional male loves his wife dearly and truly tries to please her, but is partially blinded by the Traditional patterns from his upbringing. He really is oblivious to the pleas of his wife when she asks for equal participation in social functions and household-obligations. He has egalitarian concepts but doesn't know how to apply them, in that his parents followed a Traditional pattern.

This husband says:

I go food shopping with my wife. I diaper the baby when she's gone. I watch the kids so that she can shop alone.

I put in an eight hour day. I'm tired when I come home. If she chooses to work, I won't stop her, but I expect her to take care of the kids, and keep up her household duties at the same time.

I want to watch TV evenings. She keeps interrupting my viewing with her talking. Why doesn't she get the picture when I ignore her outpourings? It makes it so hard to hear the programs. I want her by my side. It annoys me when she reads. She says she wants to share, but she's not sharing the TV with me.

Weekends, I want the family around me without outside interference. Julie says we only do what I want. I like picnics. I prefer the most isolated spot I can find every weekend. The kids enjoy the chipmunks and squirrels.

The husband continues to lament:

Julie says that the park has the same features, plus picnic tables. What's wrong with the old fashion, spread a blanket on the ground-picnic? I think it's more romantic. Julie complains of a backache. Why can't she enjoy the basic things that count?

The wife says: We both want space and time alone. Why must I do what John wants? I'm not bothering him when I read while he watches TV. Why does he feel that the rules are made by him and I must follow them? I prefer parks because I like to converse with people.

This husband's traditional blinders limit his ability to see that his wife's outside employment expands her work load into two full-time jobs so that she is working eighty to one-hundred or more hours per week. That it is his Traditional concepts of entitlement, beliefs of leisure/ recreation, and authority over family activities which allows him to ignore his wife's needs, desires, goals, and hurts. All of which causes his marriage to deteriorate. The husband believes he is acting responsibly because he selectively helps (not do them as his responsibility) his wife with what he considers are female chores.

When this type of husband acts immaturely the wife experiences the unilateral role. The Traditional role of male entitlement allows him to give himself permission to act as he wishes. The macho male is often the infantile-male. The wife has not the option to act likewise without being told how childlike she is acting. The male, who views himself as macho, rejects any female remark that he is otherwise. This denial by him, maintains his immaturity.

The female group whispers, laughs, and fume among themselves about the outrageous behavior of their little boys. You wouldn't have been drawn to read this book, HOW TO TRAIN YOUR HUSBAND TO BECOME AN ADULT if the title hadn't established a rapport with you.

Why do women accept the male definition of their roles? (Answer: It is the Traditional historical mandate.)

Why don't women define their roles? (They aren't aware that there are role obligations within each category because they were never clearly demarcated. Initially the

Traditional Roles evolved into Companionship and Partnership Roles. It's as if one accepted a position with a set of expectations only to find that additional burdens continued to be added to the original job description without prestige or monetary compensation.)

Women accept male authority because that is the male's obligation of the time-honored Traditional Role. There is no one in authority in the Partnership roles, both are equally responsible for decisions of who, what, and when things should by accomplished. Women choose the Partnership obligations and then are confused when men still select the Traditional duties. Since neither gender is aware that a selection was made, the solution is to inform both partners of the facts and and then vote on the best method to make a good marriage.

THE CON ARTIST TRADITIONAL

The Con-Artist Traditional male is well aware of the Traditional role and equal rights. He knows it is an acknowledged social role. Therefore he adheres to it because he can take advantage of gaining benefits from his wife's employment-without sharing the work load. Moreover, he can be as immature as he wishes. He pushes the limitations to the extremes and uses the dictate to play when, where, and with whatever, or whomever he wishes. He plays admittedly games.

He basks in the knowledge that he has a cultural justification of self-entitlement stipulated by Traditional roles that he has stretched to exonerate any and all of his behavior.

He says: I'm macho and I like it. I'm not about to change. She can live with it or leave it. I do what I want, when I want. If she loves me she'll want what I want. I get a big kick out of life as it is!

His attitude allows him the freedom to take up whatever role his mood determines. In his mind that does not obligate him to daily responsible behavior. In fact, he likes throwing his wife a curve. He's aware she's trying to figure him out. The more he keeps her off balance the more control he has. He is the sole determiner of his actions because traditionally the male makes all major decisions.

His wife says: He's a good man. I could have worse. I'll keep him. His wife maintains the status quo. He is under no pressure to change his attitude or his Life style. His wife vents to her woman friends to reduce her frustration. She prefers to conform to his lifestyle rather than confront him, and possibly lose the marriage.

When her husband finds out that she's disclosed their personal life to others, he's livid and forbids her to see them. He wants to continue his game. This creates a pressure cooker atmosphere. Now the wife has no where to explode, except with him.

THE CONFUSED/BORDERLINE/ PARTNERSHIP/DEVIANT TRADITIONAL

This male embraces and enjoys the aspects of equal roles by not harassing his wife for working, nor even insisting that she contribute with a salary to help maintain the home. He does not see any conflict in utilizing both the Partnership roles and the Traditional roles. However, he gives himself the right to assign which role will be served by his wife, and himself without picking up the mutual obligations that those roles demand. For example, if the wife contributes her time and income to the family's sustenance, then the corresponding duty of the husband in Partnership roles is to pick up one-half of the attending household and nurturing activities with the wife. The husband is aware of the conflicting roles and of the inequality. He may even feel a bit uncomfortable about seeing his wife overworked, but his friends laugh at his discomfort so he ignores his wife's complaints. After all he reasons he is the determiner of the rules by which they live.

Example:

Husband says: "Jim told me that his wife complains all the time, too. She wants him to help around the house and put his dirty clothes in the hamper. I really don't see why he can't do that, but I guess we men shouldn't let ourselves be de-emasculated by the wives." After all, Jim reasons they are probably only going through PMS. "Pretty soon women will expect us to jump when they want to go to the movies or visit friends. We men better stick together or we'll lose all our privileges."

The wife says: "John told me to go to work. I could keep what I make. I don't though. I want to make life easier for John. I buy the extras for the children, and my salary pays for our vacations. However it puts an overload on me with housework and all. I'm feeling more angry all the time toward him."

New guidelines need to be determined by each couple on the basis of their needs. This husband fears change that may expect that he participate cognitively and behaviorally on an adult level. That may mean that he needs to work a bit harder to create a happy-healthy relationship whose guidelines benefit both individuals plus the family, instead of being a unilateral male advantage.

THE DEVIANT TRADITIONAL

(Deviancy follows a continuum from minimal to extreme. Only the most minimal deviancy is addressed in this book.)

The Deviant Traditional male uses this role to abuse his wife with put-downs and/or obscenities. He may border on slight physical abuse which may accelerate occasionally. (The battering husband is not part of the demography for this book. Creating humor in these cases might create greater problems. Any type of abuse should be considered a serious agenda to be seen by the proper health professional for resolution.)

He says: "I only hold her down when she tries to kick me. I gave her a push. It wasn't my fault she hit her head on the table. She deserves to be told what to do. She doesn't do the right things. She undresses too fast. Is she having an affair? I'm always catching her lying. She doesn't wear an apron when she prepares dinner. What kind of a woman is that? She's lucky that I stay with her. I tell her that no other man would put up with a slut like her."

This type of man often has a co-conspiring-wife that agrees that he only meant to push her so the resulting abrasion was not the males fault. That's like saying that the drunk who drives is not responsible for killing the pedestrian because drinking and driving are two unrelated activities. The cause and responsibility for the consequences is not demanded by either spouse. Nor is normally mature behavior expected nor demanded by either partner. The wife allows, with minimal or no dissent, the husband to dictate her morals, attitudes, and goals. She lies because she's afraid of him. She isn't certain how he will twist the simple truth to reflect his devious mind. The fact that these factors constantly change to shore up the male's distorted views confuses the wife and obfuscates the issues of dissension. (The wife is not justified in hitting him either. Nor is it good common sense to take on an advisory that you can't beat.) This type of man should get professional The wife says; I should try harder. He's a good man. I feel guilty when I lose my temper. He only hit me when I hit him first.

This is not always an accurate account of the happenstance. Usually though, the woman denies the abuse because she loves him and feels that the abuse is occasional. She usually tries very hard to create a calm ambience, and actually does exceptionally well in accomplishing this. However, she berates herself because she's not perfect. Only when the violence has accelerated to hospitalization will she begin to realize that she must not accept his actions. He has choices. He can walk away when he becomes enraged. The honeymoon stage after the abuse has kept both in a denial stage preventing them from confronting reality. Moreover an enraged male frequently does not allow the women to leave. Just think about this: If a child kicks you in the shins does that give you permission to pulverize the smaller person? Are you responsible for the abrasions that result from your violence? Why is it that a woman, who is no contest for the larger male, internalizes her abuse and does not see herself as much a victim as the infant? The infant and the woman should not pick on larger predators but, does that mitigate a beating? Certainly both adults should take time out to calm down. This is the reality. Hopefully the male will allow that to happen.

Next, pick which category of behavior best describes your husband's type. Then you'll be able to determine the underlying issues. Consider the analogy of clothes. If you have never noticed a male was clothed (i.e., The roles he retained), you could never know the type of clothes he was wearing (i.e., The role-type he was). Then you can't comment on whether you agree with his style or not (i.e., The type he represents). Just as clothes determine how we react, the categorical behaviors should determine the woman's response. Consider your contemplation's if (a) a man with a black leather jacket and cap or (b) a man with a tuxedo and black patent leather shoes showed up at your door. You would ponder what objective, expectation, and plan, he was deliberating. In order to determine your reactions to the role-types you must ask yourself those same metaphorical and realistic questions and determine how that influences your actions towards him.

Now, take any of the above roles and throw in a bit of immaturity from either party, along with the normal problems of economics, in-law interference, raising children and other contingencies. (People mature their entire lives, like wine improving. Wine improves in different stages depending on the techniques and conditions in which they mature. How similar we are to wine! The levels are not always balanced. Just as some people can only make vinegar instead of wine, some people never mature.) One can see we'll need a lot jocularity to get through life.

Let's have some fun with metaphors and choose the female outfit that best conforms to your husband's. What mix and match outfit will you fashion? Females wear the appropriate attire for every occasion, why not show your spouse what kind of marriage mismatch you have by creating the the corresponding apparel?

Imagine greeting your husband at the door with the mismatched ensemble that represent the disparate obligations. A gold-lame' evening skirt (i.e., Companionship role) with a torn painted dungaree top (i.e., Equal role) and an apron over the top (representing the Traditional role). Or a Mohawk style haircut tinted orange and purple, a lion skin draped over your nude body and bare feet to represent the Deviant Traditional role. Let your fanciful funny bone take over. (I suggest a wig for the hair style.)

Whether you care to represent the scrambled marital roles by corresponding clothing or not matters less than the shared awareness that a mix and match outfit exists. This material not only illuminates the classification which most resembles your life style, but establishes an awareness that couples may re-negotiate their lifestyles to fit their personal preferences, instead of personalizing their differences in deliberate antagonistic actions. In most situations, the husband has subliminally reacted to his perceptions of society, which as every woman knows is not the same as the female's viewpoint.

Women's freedom originated with our right to vote in the 1920's. That barely began equal rights. Freedom has to filter into the hearts and minds and change internal attitudes before there is true liberation.

The "Spoiled Child" Chapter describes the history that separates and distorts genders beyond the "It's a Boy" concept.

The spoiled child certainly is not always the abuser, but with certain attributes and cultural dictates, some individuals could be led more easily in that direction.

Spoiling advances immaturity. An immature person is a good target for developing deviancy, and/or narcissistic type behavior.

CHAPTER 19
THE SPOILED CHILD

(Do frogs spoil their offspring?)

"I want." and the response, "Let me get it for you," are human sentiments, and as such cause no problem. However, if several times a day, day in and day out, past infancy into teen years, these desires are fulfilled as if the individual were still a baby; the resulting youth is damaged by the lack of boundaries in his/her world. The mounting insecurities developed because the family's world allows unrestricted license to surpass the rights of others, contrasted with the restrictions at school which could create a warped personality. Narcissistic, deviant, immature, demanding, and blaming are the likely result of the grown children's discordant behaviors as a result of coddling by parents. (This does not always happen for many reason not addressed here.)

Parents spoil because they're not knowledgeable about child-rearing techniques.

They do not consider the long term consequences of their over indulgences. Parents spoil because they're overburdened by life's adversities and want to eliminate a child's screams as a stressor. Parent's spoil because they feel they must give everything to their child because they never had it. Parents spoil because they value the child's life over their own, therefore granting entitlements (that, perhaps, were denied them in their childhood) that should never be given. Some parents spoil because they feel inadequate and they fear they'll lose their children's love. Some parents might spoil a child because the parent(s) feel guilty about some lifestyle circumstance such as divorce. Guilt is the motivating factor in many of these situations.

A spoiled person has an self-image of perfection while sensing that a rotten core lies within. Addictive personalities result from a conception of an internalized monster lurking to attack in the form of obsessive outlets such as: overworking, overeating, alcohol, drugs,and/or sex. Patrick Carnes's books on addiction have more to add on the subject of addiction. moreover the spoiled adult, blames everyone except himself (or herself) for every unpleasant happening. The spoiled adult is impossible to live with, and close to impossible to counsel.

The requirements of change are:

A recognition of the problem source.

Accepting responsibility for altering one's own behavior which is directly linked as a cause that creates an effect.

Understanding the dynamic that suffering motivates change.

Perseverance to work step by step to bring about a resolution.

Most damaged personalities lack the recognition or the responsibility to own their problem.

They blame their unhappiness on other people. They are not committed to finding a solution. Therefore, the suffering they feel is free-floating. The necessary connection that would bring about an answer is not available to them. Nor is the ability to persevere prevalent because the pampered person has never developed the patience to wait, to accomplish an aim because everything has been given to him/her, even before it was asked.

(Again since we are directing this book towards men, that gender will be used to further describe the problems of spoiling.)

There is always a built in limit somewhere. Usually the desires exceed the resources about the time that a youth becomes a teenager. Then the teenager becomes frustrated because he isn't given the car he wants. As the teenager reaches adulthood the anger escalates. In adulthood, the wife becomes the target when she can't provide eternal happiness for this physically overdeveloped child.

(Remember the example of the man who wanted his house cleaned and sex simultaneously? Come to think of it. That would be kinky sex.)

Part of the bonding that bind women to these men is a subconscious recognition of that tiny unhappy child within the raging man because she has a biological and cultural mandate to fulfill her maternal instinct.

The wife states: I should hate him for battering me, but I love him. I can't leave him.

However, the likelihood of reversing adverse personality traits for either sex is very unlikely. Miracles don't happen often, but if you know of one, don't write the author to tell me I'm wrong. Instead, go down on your knees and pray to

God that he graced the both of you. I am happy for your good fortune.

That doesn't mean a person can't modify his behavior. Moreover, not all the deviancy results from any one component. Any one of these: The cultural traditional duties, improper upbringing, malfunctioning neurological components, or the biological mandates of the the DNA which determines fifty-five to sixty-five percent of inborn-personality; may be the cause of the aberration.

Conversely, biological differences might even be the saving grace that aids a person to surpass the vagaries of one's upbringing.

Spare the rod and spoil the child has a bit of truth to it. Children need discipline. Discipline need not be physical, nor abusive, but loving, consistent, and supervisory to organize the child's life. A youth needs to understand the limits of obnoxious behavior. A male adult also needs boundaries.

Sending him to his room for one minute as often as needed will do the trick. Think about how long one minute feels when you are waiting for a traffic light to change. One minute is a long enough time for the many trivial transgressions. However, wait until your child stops screaming and throwing things before the one minute discipline begins. Then start the time clock, when the one minute elapses; call your child from his room. If the next tantrum is one second later, repeat as often as necessary the one minute discipline. Often children will realize that you are gaining control over them, and initially will increase delinquent behaviors. However, consistent and persistent discipline will win out (usually within a month). Consistent, persistent neutrality and a humorous manner of informing your husband of his behaviors, will also win out over your spoiled husband/child.

Moreover, continual supervising so that the youth follows through on whatever you have stipulated to be done decreases adverse behavior. Take an extra moment to stop housecleaning, and see if he has picked up his room. If not, give a second reminder. Again check, if the room is not being worked on, then apply discipline. In time the child will respond by the first command. The youth feels loved because not only has he received attention constantly, but has the security of boundaries that effectively guide actions which bring him acclaim. Your husband also needs specific guidelines.

Decide on the guide lines together. Specify your expectations in order that he can please you.

For example: I was doing the accounting for my business, and at the same time I was co- ordinating everything that I must accomplish. I had six hours of counseling appointments to begin within the next twenty minutes. The kitchen floor needed scrubbing, and the laundry had to be done. I felt like I wished to scream obscenities at my husband who was sitting watching me work, when I realized I must follow my own advice to specify what I needed to be done. I explained to my husband that in lieu of diamonds and furs, his co-operation on household duties signified to me that he loved me. Then, I reviewed my list mentally and decided that I could request that he do the wash, since he had done it on a past occasion. He said, "Sure Honey," and completed the job. I hadn't verbalized my anger, but had spoken evenly. I was pleased with the results. However, if your husband responds with, "Do it yourself," you will need a different approach.

Children intimidate their parents with their confrontational style. (A child is small. What about a two hundred pound man being confrontational?). Insecure adults will give in to a child who says, "I hate you!" or "All the other kid's parents let them do it!" These parents need guidance to deal with their own inadequacies in order that they might feel strong enough to insist that their offspring follow their rules. Just as a woman needs to feel un-coerced when requesting her husband's co-operation. Guidelines develop mature goals of happiness, responsibility, and sensitivity toward others with marriage and with parenting. It takes strength to say no to the child within your husband when he has acted out in the same manner as your children. Try misinterpreting the husband's "Do it yourself". Roll your eyes coyly and respond, "It's more fun to do it together!" This insinuates that co-operation in every aspect of marriage begets rewards. (Some females are so resentful that they will take offense to this suggestion. They feel that they are prostituting themselves. I am suggesting that they let go of the anger and look for solutions. Teasing, caring, and sharing bring more rewarding results.)

There is a lack of discipline and a lack of consequences in the upbringing of a spoiled individual. These persons may not respond to any type of motivation. Regardless of the reasons that parents spoil their sons, whether it was because he was the special male gender, or other reasons is immaterial. What is important is the resulting three year old personality who can kick you and not feel a thing, but wonder why you screamed. Now you as an adult are left to raise your husband. The paradox is that unless he disciplines himself, you'll always have a perpetual child. The solution? Help him through whimsy to realize his childish ways.

Buy him a pacifier. (Just kidding.)

CHAPTER 20
BACK TO THE THEME- ROCK-A-BYE-
BABY

(He is a huge Bullfrog!)

The Deviant Traditional role model has been viewed from a number of contexts.

This Chapter deals with abusive rearing which propagates identical behavior towards the following generations becoming intergenerational abuse. It is another example of the Deviant Traditional Role model.

If abusive situations don't apply to your life skip this, but as a matter of interest you might read on anyway.

Let's explore the upcoming theme of bringing up hubby by assessing a nursery song:

Rock-a-bye baby on the tree top when the wind blows the cradle will rock when the bough breaks the cradle will fall and down will come baby, cradle and all.

That is a very hostile song. Did the mother wish the baby to fall? Why put the baby in the treetop? It's even saying rock a bye, which could be interpreted; good by to baby, let's get rid of the kid. Infanticide. Amazing! We sing this to our infants. !t was song to us. We never think about what the words might signify to a child. Only the mentally unbalanced parent would follow through with that intent. Let's face it, kids can get your goat. Yet some deviant adults physically and verbally harass their children just because they were born. Or is it that the responsibility is more than some overtaxed parents can handle? Did your husbands upbringing scar him?

What is the right way to raise the next generation? If your parents were abusive where do you learn how to establish correct parenting patterns?

If you only know the wrong way, that question can be overwhelming and unanswerable, such as in the following example:

You can scream at your child in the supermarket to shut the kid up. When that doesn't work you can slam him one for screaming. Now that will shut him up! It didn't? He screamed louder? Well how is it that the check-out persons heard a child crying, a mother screaming, "Shut up!" as a slap connected with the child's face or butt. If people are unable to contain themselves in a public places, imagine how the youth's head rolls in private.

(Because of the CPS crack down that is seldom witnessed in public any more. It does not mean that privately the parents are under control.)

How is it that all these adults can't figure out cause and effect? These adults were once in the same position, and now as parents they are automatically repeating the older generations mistakes; word for word, blow for blow. Amazingly they feel the same anger, frustration, exhaustion, and lack of patience which their parents felt. If they would stop and listen to themselves they would recognize the exact phrases that they heard as a youth. That would be the first step towards correcting that behavior. The youngsters felt unloved as they were intimidated. They react with timidity, or blasting when they were rebellious. They are now the Moms and Dads. These parents are treating their loved ones precisely as they were disciplined.

How do we begin a new world order? Where does it end? Do we shake an accusing head at the greyed hair generation, who now pamper their grandchildren? (Most great grandparents are not aware they erred. "That's how I was brought up. I turned out Al right didn't I?, they'll say to you if you ask.) In the 1900's psychologists and sociologists began investigating the results of child rearing on behavior.

Everything got blamed on the environment. Now we know that 60% of behavior is programmed by DNA and only 40% is upbringing, but that 40% can be nearly lethal.

Erik Erickson's stages of development of trust and autonomy in the early years can be badly destroyed by a father (or mother) who yells profanities at an infant; "You f----ing brat Get your s--- face over here. The child knocked over his milk. The parents react as if the crown jewels had just been stolen. The room isn't neat. It's treated as a major catastrophe.

As the child grows he is scalded with expletives that, if ever used, could only be used on one's worst enemies, but some children hear them all. The father who is tired, worried about finances, or angry that his wife is pregnant again (even though he enjoyed that process) takes his anger out on safe targets. (Or today-anger is generated from the economic crisis of losing ones job and home.) (The children can not fight back.

They feel they're responsible but deep inside they know that that is unfair.

Now that child is a man. He is bitching at his wife. These are some of his accusations:.

"Can't you keep the house clean? Where is the belt I told you to buy for me? What do you do all day? Coffee-Klatch?" Your husband just became his father and the wife is now the victim, as he was, when Dad vented all his frustrations on him. Your husband is so out of touch with his feelings that he'd have another tantrum if you told him exactly what it was that he was experiencing.

Tantrums. You as a mother are familiar with infantile tantrums. If the toddler wanders from you, the child is happy. However, if you go out of sight the child's security is shaken. The child screams.

Tantrums. Lack of security. Aborted stages of trust and development. This is where rage can stem. With such a background, how does one begin again? That's a good question, because without your hubby's co-operation, it's unlikely there will be change.

Capricious illustrations might enlighten one towards maturity. One woman was reminded of her child's tantrums. She lay on the floor flaying her extremities. Her husband said, "Have you gone crazy?" "No," she said, "I thought I'd emulate your behavior so you could see what you look like to me when you are having a fit."

Another wife responded to her husband's rage with a quiet neutral voice, "Your day must have been horrendous! Why don't you share it with me!" He denied that anything happened to upset him and continued to harass her. She suggested that he go out and play and return when he was in a better mood.

Of course if he has recently returned from playing at the local bar, suggesting that he return there is akin to telling your child to go play in the traffic.

Just as the wife must respond with firm quieting tones to her little ones in the supermarket, she might motivate the child by promising a game as soon as the groceries are put away. Then live up to her promise. She, also must respond in normal tones to her husband.

But what games can she promise a man? Sex? Well then, the woman becomes a prostitute, if she uses sex to siphon off the males anger. Sex should be a shared loving experience. How does the male feel about sex?

Let's imagine his comments.

"She owes it to me."

"I'm a normal male. I'm unsatisfied because she has a headache, is sick, or isn't in the mood."

"It's a wife's duty."

"I'll have to look elsewhere if you aren't ready soon."

"I'm tired of waiting. I want a divorce."

"There's something wrong with you. You'd better get it fixed-fast."

"You must be getting it somewhere else. If I find him I'll rip his b----s off."

Compare this to your child's remarks when you refuse him a candy bar.

"All the other mother's give their kids an allowance so they can get candy whenever they want." is similar to the attitude, "She owes it to me".

The husband believes that his wife is capable of performing, but won't, therefore this is the basis for his accusation. The child states his demands: "Why don't you have any money? I saw you put it in the bank."

The kid says, "I had to borrow a candy bar from my friend, you'll have to pay him back." The husband accepts no responsibility for his actions. It never occurs to him that his intimacy skills are in poor repair.

"It's your duty to take care of me because I'm a kid." Husband: My wife owes me happiness.

The kid says: "I'll run away if you don't give me what I want." But, the husband can run away and states, "I want a divorce."

Did you ever see so many similarities in requests? Whose learning from whom? Why does a man's comments, threats, and manipulations sound like a twelve year old?

Why don't women recognize the strategies when they come from an adult? He is expected to be mature. Therefore his actions are considered threatening.

If sex is a women's duty, then it becomes work. Work means we agree that during certain hours we lose our freedom to choose other activities. Loss of freedom to spontaneously react to shared love making is gone and a rigid demand takes its place, destroying the fun of lovemaking. Making sex becomes a F——ing. That is right! It makes it an obscene word which lacks caring consideration, mutual respect, and agreement.

Masked or open threats are one step from rape. They are verbal rape. Blaming the wife for not being available for the husband's entertainment is manipulation. The wife often believes the male when he says fix it, fast. Why should the wife try? Is there anything for her to repair? Occasionally she might have a hormonal deficiency, especially after delivering a child. However the likelihood is that the wife has lost interest because she has accepted the messages that she must perform when she is not in the mood. Sex is an appetite. A person will restrain self- moderated appetites in order to establish a sense of power. Women might limit food (anorexia) or might limit sex. Unfortunately she might transfer her need for love by taking a bit of of the only kind of power she can get by excessively eating, or shopping. People stripped of control will garner whatever arena that is open to them.

Alternatively, one might try establishing acceptable boundaries for oneself and for ones mate. When a woman is able to identify the real issues, she can give herself further permission to take complete control constructively. Women can govern their lives by compiling a list of other options. Then she might study all the components of her marital relationship. Once this is accomplished, utilize the list to develop enhanced family moments that unify each moment into pleasure, which is akin to laughter.

Within the list one should include:

1. Determining the real issue.

2. Specify clearly each need and boundary.

3. Compile humorous responses and thoughts to break tension and redirect goals.

4. Engage a marital counselor if the above items can not be accomplished.

5. Protect yourself from violence. Seek a county shelter, the police, or any other legal means so that you are not abused.

Women who read this book and decide that it is foreign to their personality; are probably resisting the entitlements which they deserve. (Or hopefully, they do not have these horrendous situations in their life.)

Women are waiting for men to grant them permission to have rights.

Women, instead must stand up for their rights, because they are mature adults.

Chapter 21 outlines the basis for women's trepidation, next.

CHAPTER 21

WOMEN UNITE

(Now as the Princess, not the frog.)

Women are adults. They can limit or determine their own selections, but some feel they have no control over any part of their life. Unless ladies return self-government to themselves their freedom is restricted by their own internalized messages absorbed from the outdated cultural Traditional Role obligations. How sad. They have accepted the blame that parents, men, and the society have heaped on them. Wives are not even aware that they are giving their mate permission to control them instead of taking control of their own destiny.

Holding the power in a women's life means recognizing the verbal/ taboo chains that shackle females. These chains: are subliminal guilt trips that a woman must accept the entire effort to make a relationship run smoothly.

She internalizes these messages as: It must be something I've done or forgot to do. This bondage keeps women at the co-conspiracy level of balancing the Traditional role model which sometimes results in deviances.

(Women misusing the controlling power also destroys marriages.)

For example Here is a guilt message:

Mom and Dad always said, "You are in control of your destiny. What have you done? Why haven't you more friends?" This is a double bind message. They empower her only to then suggest that she has misused it in some undefined manner.

Identify the source of your messages. In the above case, it is the parents. The guilt may be dictated from your parents, your religion, from your peers, from the Traditional role obligation, or from your own decisions based on any of these directives. After identifying the source, ask yourself, "Does this dictate improve my life or destroy it?"

Give yourself permission to refuse to accept the blame for everything that happens. Sort what is your responsibility and what is the obligation of the other person.

For example:

Is it your fault your husband didn't eat his lunch?

He says: You didn't put my lunch out where I could remember to bring it with me.

What does she say? "Yes dear?" or she could say, "When you get hungry enough times, you'll recall that food is stored in the refrigerator so it won't spoil." Only if she is released from the cultural nurturing dictates will she respond in the latter manner.

Eliminating the self-blame is often the most difficult, because the message is a subconscious tape recording that replays itself. Identify the offending message. Then Imagine that you are erasing the recording. Push the erase button in your brain. Erase the damaging missive.

Replace the guilt with realistic messages, such as: This is his problem. I'll back off and let him handle it.

Once women release these restraints, they can refuse blame or responsibility for someone's happiness. Women can insist that the shared lovemaking be created by a romantic ambience which both partners mutually develop. We called it courtship when we first met our beau's. Throughout marriage there should be a responsive courtship.

Men were taught to court, but with marriage they end it. Recently scientists have found that

during courtship men have the hormone, which creates happy secure feelings. After marriage, the disappears from their system.

Women, through fairy tales that begin with a Cinderella wedding costume, obtain the opposite message.

To break these sanctions, both genders must be aware of them and be willing to cooperate toward maintaining a romantic relationship for the duration of their life and marriage. One can make a date with ones spouse, dress for it, make time for it, and establish an activity that both find pleasurable. Just as dates do not always terminate in lovemaking, inform your husband to not anticipate that all his trysts will end with that sequence. The goal is to set the mood by creating the ambience, not forcing it into a date rape situation.

Women have to demand respect. Study your husband's requests. He insists that you respect him. Let him know that you will respond to shared respect.

For example is he disrespectful of you? He walks by the sink and remarks, "I

notice the dishes aren't done yet?"
When have you walked by the kitchen
sink and made a remark even vaguely
similar? If the couple are both equally
employed full time why can't you say
that? He says it. Do you?

Women have to respect their own
needs and their own persons. If a
women cringes while considering this
action, then she is acting as if she were
the child in the relationship. Respond in
a childlike manner, and you will be
treated as one.

She says: I can't tell him what I feel. He
won't talk to me for days. She doesn't
want to stand up to him and challenge
his assertion of rights. Now the wife is
the mother to her husband because she
is nurturing him, but is also his child
because she is following his directive.
Confusing? No wonder females have
difficulty untangling relationships. The
husband is both the child and the
authority figure for the family. I thought I
would throw that in to illustrate how
confusing it is for everyone.

When a ten year old child is losing in a game, he wants to change the rules for himself, but for no one else. If the rules change for everyone, then it is fair. The rules changed for women when the Traditional Roles also included the equal obligation of supporting the family (the former male role) without the equivalent participation of sharing responsibilities from the husbands. (This is made equal in many families, now, but this book is not addressing issues that have been modified, but, rather issues that are still unchanged with the transforming times.)

The entire mess can be sorted out on a psychological level also, when we utilize a (TA) transactional analysis theory. Every person has three ego states as Eric Berne pointed out: a Parent who instructs us (our conscience), an Adult that sorts the facts, and a Child who

emotionally responds to situations. If someone speaks to us from the parental (authority) level we usually respond from the child level with resentment. Therefore whenever a person commands, the other usually rebels, at least internally. A refusal to talk or act in co-ordination with the others desires is passive resistance which is another form of rebellion.

For example: Martha's husband, John, takes a piece of pie from her, as she is putting a forkful to her mouth, and says, "You're supposed to be dieting." The child within Martha rebels. She consumes the entire pie as soon as he leaves the house, even though she's acting contrary to her wishes to remain on a diet. When angry, John will eat an apple pie instead of lunch to assert his inner child. Both examples show the emotional reactions which is the internal child level of the personality.

Analyzing the ego-stage that each partner is acting out helps to define the situation in order to resolve it. For instance, a woman might use the adult-part of her ego to decide what type of inter reaction exchange is taking place.

She might respond to the child within the male by letting him know that she acknowledges that he requires attention and appreciation. She might stroke his hair, kiss him, relate an attractive feature about him that she loves, and then let him know that she is legitimately tired this evening, but will rest and make time for his love making, hopefully the next evening.

The stroking appeals to the child within him. The facts are directed toward his intellectual self, the adult ego state. If the male is not ready to deal at the adult-level, then the female must return to listening and understanding what the male is feeling. This is active listening that is used by Counselor's. It is a communication skill that works with all ages. It is not pampering, nor is it demeaning, since the control of the circumstance is with the individual who understands the dynamics of relationship.

Once the above is accomplished satisfactorily, then resolve the situation.

In this case the solution would be to make a date with him to share a pleasant day or night. Both parties must pace their schedule, so that they may be rested sufficiently to enjoy the evening.

However, what techniques will help the female to convince the male to join her? The woman needs to suggest that they establish a plan that they could both share. Females will probably take this as the same old game-plan. She does all the work preparing for an agreed-upon party and the male merely shows up.

Wrong!! Request help. Just as when you want your child to learn responsible behavior, you give him/her definitive activities, such as:

Please take out the garbage when you see it piled up, put your socks in the hamper each and every time you take them off, eat only at the table as the crumbs create additional vacuuming for me.

To train a hubby you need to direct your attention to detailed-not general deeds which need to be done:

"Underclothes which we need to wear tonight have not been laundered as yet. I haven't the time to do it. I'm preparing dinner for our guests. If I to do it, we won't be eating," is a fact not a command.

It can be followed by a request, "Would you see to it? Please? Your wardrobe has not been checked by me to see if everything is clean and has all the buttons," is presenting information.

"We have one hour to get ready," states more facts.

"I notice you haven't shaved yet," is a comment not a command. However, it could be misconstrued as "You should have shaved by now." If that is the case for you, alter your comment to, "We have only one hour to get ready. In the past you have waited until I am ready before you shave. I get annoyed because now we are gong to be late."

Those comments follow the Behavior, Feeling, Effect requirements. Usually messages that imply no guilt which are factual, bring better results from the other person.

These are not parenting messages,. They actuality allow the individual to have the final vote in deciding whether to act upon the data. Complete, accurate reporting aids the other person's assessment misusing and encourages co-operation.

Is the more sharing communication skills necessary? Yes, if in the past, your husband has waited by the door complaining that you take forever, as your dress yourself, dress the infants, prepare the food, and so forth. Just as you are finally leaving, he remembers that he must shave and delays the entire family. Again facts must be delivered in a neutral manner that report, (when the other message is ignored) the effect that the wife has readied three people, herself and two children, while he spent his time complaining.

The wife might say:

I'm running a three ring circus here, feel free to jump in and take over any job you wish. There are the acting jobs of happiness, the producing job of co-ordinating people, food preparation, and costumes to be put on. Which performance would you like to participate with so that we can get ready quicker?

If the male has adult reasoning available within his three-ego-states, he will acknowledge that he has acted in a childish manner. The husband has not been reliable, even for himself. However the Traditional male views himself as loyal by going to work, supporting his family, and doing traditionally masculine jobs such as mowing the lawn and fixing the car.

Often, his behavior mimics your eight year old daughter's when she purchases you a game she loves to play. Does your husband give you a fishing pole for Christmas, knowing you'll never kill a fly, let alone a fish? Why not buy him the new_____. (You fill in the blank, e.g. perfume that you always wanted). When he wonders why you gave him something so feminine, point out to him that the fishing pole is too masculine for you. Let him know that you were trying to get him to realize that he is purchasing what he wants in the same way as you did.

If his spending prevents you from having money for your needs, you must have a serious talk with him on an adult to adult level. Or open a separate account to match his, in order to emphasize his unilateral actions by a duplication of his. When he notices, let him know your reasons for your action. Discuss what behaviors need to change for you to rejoin him as a unit.

Does your husband spend all the money so that when the tot's school clothes must be purchased, there is nothing left except for your earnings? Try quipping with him. You might say to the spouse (who has purchased the third fishing reel when he hasn't used the first one yet) "I love toys too, but there's not enough fish for dinner tonight." If a gibe remark doesn't jog the male, then return to more serious talk which establishes guidelines that apply to both parties.

A budget that places finances aside for house, family, medical, educational, and couple shared expenses, should be jointly contributed to and withdrawn from. As soon as either party notices that an expense is higher than anticipated, another conference should be held to re-establish new terms. Run your home as you would a business. After the bills are paid, then each of you might want to draw an equal-share of the remainder.

If there is no remainder, go over the budget for expenses that are not necessary, or that could be pruned. Both spouses should have an equal share for luxury items. The fact that an addiction (such as smoking) is not controllable does not change the truth that one person is exceeding the budget for unilateral needs.

Pruning the budget to cover necessities might free up a few dollars. If the definition of the word budget insults either of you, solve it by defining it as a roof over your head, clothes for the

proper seasons, food, and education. Those are basics. Expenses can be limited. A house needs to be leak proof, but it needn't be a palace. Use logic to determine the circumstances.

For example:

One farmer insisted his city-bride wear the only type of shoes she owned into the chicken coop to collect eggs. The fact that the shoes were high heels did not give him pause. He was lucky his bride divorced him before she needed traction from slipping on the chicken manure. Obviously the groom had a skewed sense of economy, especially since he'd just spent money on some artistic doodads. Logistical priorities must be used to determine a budget.

However if you are unable to declare your rights, you need to review what you feel you are entitled to in life. Have you ever said, "My husband won't let me," and meant it? (Women traditionally withdraw from any type of conflict.) If you have, give yourself this test. Answer yes or no. Take the test for the fun of it. It might enlighten you.

Do you feel you have the right to be equal with men, as well as, women?

Do you feel you have the right to verbalize a disagreement?

Do you feel you have the right to be accepted including your imperfections and strengths?

Will you accept a confrontation to air your rights and grievances? Do you release yourself from the traditional role dictates?

Do you feel you have the right to make your own choices?

Do you respect yourself? (i.e. Do you make decisions that align with your morals and goals so that you feel inner peace?)

Do you feel you have the right to restructure your life according to your own life's blueprint? Do you feel you are contributing to society?

Are you allowing your husband these same rights?

If the answer to some or all of the above questions is negative then you need to re-examine why and how you have reached a point in your life where you are nothing but a welcome mat for everyone to wipe their feet on. Every answer to the above questions should be yes.

Every adult, regardless of sex requires structured personal guidelines. In order to have self- esteem one must improve the society in which one resides, speak up for ones values, and verbalize ones requirements. Without these prerequisites a person does not mature. However, maturing is not satisfying your desires at the expense of others. What are your values? Sensitivity, Loyalty, Education?

Write your list if you are not in touch with what takes prominence in your life.

It is important to prioritize minor annoyances from major issues. For instance: Would you be upset if your husband fixed the roof instead of buying you a birthday gift? What if there was only enough money for one expense? Would it have been improvident to let the roof leak? Has he really ignored you? Handle a petty issue on that level without blowing it non-proportionally high. In the above case, the wife might request some fun that is cost-free to celebrate her specialness. After the problem is resolved, let the angry feelings blow off in the wind, and then go on to more significant issues.

There is a hidden secret in this book and it is that no one can control anyone except themselves. Between you and me no one can train anyone, only themselves. Woman need to discover how they can become better people, so that the frogs in their lives can live-up to the improved standards that woman will portray.

Women can build self-confidence by performing tasks which ordinarily would require a man's participation. The library is filled with self-help books to couch anyone in any field. Adult and college courses are available to educate either gender in unfamiliar areas. Once a person completes gender-chores satisfactorily they experience self-confidence and a sense of self-reliance and independence that bolsters one's sense of self-worth. (The confidence level of the female soldiers that were engaged in the Iraqi/Allied Coalition Way must have had them flying high.)

Taking public speaking courses will organize thinking skills and break through the wall of non-expression. Joining debate teams will help develop extemporaneous thinking that facilitates verbal agility. Even more importantly, women must allow and make room for at least twenty minutes a day to develop their own potential separately from their mate. That could be relaxing, reading, exercising, pursuing a hobby, or an education.

Divorcees and widows need to prepare themselves for every eventuality to handle life alone. It requires women to be capable, organized, and independently able to maintain themselves economically. Both genders most attempt to live up to their best potential.

After the female has conquered the lack of self-confidence she should be ably prepared to discuss gender and marital differences with the male.

There is one last hurdle for the female to conquer and that is fear of the consequences in airing her opinions.

Women need to determine whether they are the victim of actual violent circumstances. If she has felt a physical or mental onslaught of rage, she may well hesitate to convey her dissatisfactions.

Emotionally or physically abused women must consider their options:

Leave.

Insist on professional counseling for each separately, and together.

Attempt a non-confrontational communication.

A combination of any of the above.

(The author hopes the victim does not choose this option.) Put up with it-- which possibly can result in endangering her life and those of her children.

Prayerfully, the victim will give herself the right to remove herself and any others affected until the violator has sought help; and has rescinded all his attitudes and actions that would harm any member of the family.

However, if you have evaluated your husband's actions and find that your fears have no significance, then explore your background in order to discover the source of your rationalization. Were your parent(s) nurturing verbally or physically abusive? Was there any authority (teacher, religious leader, relative, older person or sibling) which overwhelmed your coping skills during your childhood?

Do you recall ever promising yourself that it is better to remain silent than bring the wrath of an adult down upon yourself? Can you remember when this happened and who motivated the reaction? Now as an adult you are stuck at that age level whenever there is a conflict. Connect with this child within yourself and nurture her.

Perhaps past coping skills worked for you as a minor, but resolutions are not reached unless you voice your thoughts. Many marriages crumble because of the accumulated resentment of the past's unresolved incidents. Unresolved incidents are often those issues which have never been aired.

For example:

After ten years of marriage she says: I sacrificed my time to go visit your parents when I didn't want to go.

He says: I'm not a mind reader. How did I know?

She realizes that he's not a psychic. She laughs and says: I expect my prince charming to read my mind.

Admitting fallibility's relieves the tension, makes us chuckle and creates a pleasant bonding. In the following example the wife gives clear specific suggestions to advance a solution.

She says: How is it that I am doing men's work by being employed outside the home? I expect you to sacrifice some of your time helping me prepare dinner after we've both worked all day.

He says: I don't like to do that.

She says: It doesn't make my day either. Put on the wash, dust the furniture. Take your pick. I work as many hours as you at work, and then put in another work week at home.

He says: But it's a women's job.

She says: I can do everything myself, but if I do that, I may as well be single again.

Women need to let men know what their expectations are; in order to have men conform to them. Gender tasks based on the Traditional role that certain duties belong to one sex or the other causes men to wear blinders as they walk through a dusty, messy, home because the woman is employed outside the home and hasn't the time to accomplish both jobs. Males, do not see the duties as significant, do not feel obliged to perform household tasks.

The Traditional role never included outside employment. Some men don't acknowledge housework as work, often their lives do not change significantly when a women is employed. Therefore, they continue to wear blinders. However the women who refuse to accept both the Equal role of sharing the economic burden and the Traditional role that includes every other responsibility, will spark their partner into sharing the load. The frightened woman who continues to bear the burden of all the roles, and does not speak her frustration is stuck in a marriage that is deteriorating. There are exceptions of course, where a minority of women prefer to live by the Traditional roles. If you are satisfied with your role, then why are you reading this book?

Often women (accept all the marital requirements from various role models, and then are angry with the men who they believe have callously refused to be supportive. When a woman overcomes her fear, and gives herself equal-rights, she no longer gunny sacks her frustrations: but openly airs them and most importantly the confrontations are resolved which creates a satisfying relationship.

Comical remarks create an acceptable distance that aids the woman to alleviate her fears. In a sense, she can hide behind her wit, should her mate take offense to her remarks.

In case of any type of withdrawal (walking away, silence, etc.). Allow it. Ask only for a schedule of when the person will be ready to have a discussion. Be prepared to give facts, and feelings and allow your partner equal time to do the same.

Once you) have succeeded with good natured whimsy in allowing yourself to obtain your husband's co-operation in all endeavors, you can utilize the following process:

Obtain your husband's attention.

Together imagine goals that would
continue the rebuilding process.

Schedule advantageous times for
discussion/appointments.

Then practice good communication
skills that specify needs, wants, goals,
values.

Give equal time for both to air their
opinions.

Match equal listening time to hear
complaints.

Vent as soon as there is a problem, for
minor events and make appointments
for major

problems so that the situation may be
explored adequately.

8. Ask for additional information continually as an ongoing process about the others feelings, facts, and opinions.

9. Take time out when the atmosphere becomes too heated.

10. Establish solutions. For example: Together decide on guidelines such as determining each persons most irritable times and allowing each other non-confrontational periods during those times.

Each couple's guidelines will be based on their own idiosyncrasies. So each set of couples must determine their own guidelines. A list made out by each spouse will help identify specific patterns that need attention.

For example:

The husband wants to relax for one hour after work in order to change gears. His wife doesn't like to talk when she arises. After discovering these limitations about each other, they decide to have one hour silent time in the morning and after work. Their children are apprised of this arrangement. Life goes on more smoothly since everyone knows the other's need for time-outs.

11. The next step is to activate the process and maintain your guidelines daily.

12. Then step-back and observe the ongoing process.

13. If it bogs down, express your disappointment and repeat the process until you have a fortuitous conclusion.

Remember to restructure the situation as Tak did with Mal reframing with wit assists with depleting tension and establishing non threatening resolutions.

GOOD LUCK!

Chapter 22 offers step by step behaviors to lead the reader to learn how to develop their funny- bone.

Formulas, fairy tales for adults, fanciful playing with words, ideas, and concepts, creates the atmosphere for amusement.

A return to the frog theme, plus more stories which will guide you to a plan for happiness.

CHAPTER 22

RETURN OF THE FROGS

A strange phenomenon is happening as the ballroom strobe light flashes intermittently. What is seen is a Frog metamorphosing into a Prince, another Frog transforming into a Princess.

Flash...Frog-Princess-Frog-Prince.
Flash...Frog-Princess, Frog-Prince.
Flash...

But, some of these are reversed:

Flash...Princess-Frog, Prince-Frog.
Flash...Prince-Frog, Princess-Frog,..Flash...

It is unnerving to be your highness one moment, and then the next moment a swamp frog. However, after fifty years of ballroom dancing, the Frog phenomenon apparently goes on unobserved. The frog leaping without advance notice shakes the Kingdom because frogs are now in control creating a Frog-doom. Just when the Prince and Princess have become extremely secure that they have mastered the art of being supreme, they are reminded of their roots. They must be always monitor their actions of empathy towards others or the ugly side takes precedence.

As their Kingdom becomes more securely theirs with infrequent flashes of the darker side, they are able to establish another unusual wonder. There are only two kinds of beings in their dominion: frogs or royalty. There is an equality among the many Prince and Princesses. The sovereignty reigned, observing frogs in every stage that they themselves had grown through. Some frogs where leaping over each other with grace. But, others were deliberately grinding their hind legs into the eyes of the other less fortunate, forcing them to lose the race. The winners were surprised to find that they were the losers. The majesties enabled the vanquished to find fresh water and ignored the crafty competitors.

Other co-conspirators tried nudging victims into corners where they could become the prey of predators. The trapped victims sang courageous songs. Another strange thing happened, the raptors, attracted by the song, became entangled with them. Some of the victims joined forces with both warring sides in order to save themselves.

The royal couple felt sorry for the vanquished, but that didn't grant them a royal entrance. Especially those confused frogs who replayed their victimization out on others in an attempt to figure out why they had been captured. However, those tadpoles who comprehended that the cycle of unpleasant actions must end, revitalized kind candidates to add to the the nobility. Those lucky frogs realized that the altruistic ones inspired the respect of others. What a paradox! The more the villains fought for Princedom the more entrenched they became in Frog- doom. (One can not fight for love. One can only express love to gain love.) The Royal couple loved all the frogs, even the ruffians. They enjoyed watching their clumsy stages of development. They knew that all the frogs meant well, but some lost the path because they had whipped up so much mud upon them that they couldn't see it. They would find their way. At least that is what the regal twosome hoped. They would say, "Watch out!" occasionally, but mostly they would step aside and await the reformation from tad poles to Royalty.

The fairy tale generates a frolicsome atmosphere. Playing releases tension and incubates joy, amusement, and Humor. Pleasant feelings, mirth-loving ways opens the curiosity door to answers. Buoyancy includes others. However, put-downs is an exercise in exclusion and will work in reverse. Cheerfulness creates a vehicle for each family member to state their emotions

without endangering the other
members.

Develop a story line that recreates your
history of your courtship, your wedding,
your daily life, and dramatic events that
intersperse your life. Emphasize the
extremes, the paradoxes, and the
absurdities for the Humor-accent. It
might film something like this:

TYPE OF COURTSHIP:

We met at the end of grocery lines. We
were the child in tow of our parents. At
graduation we were the last male and
female to match as we ceremoniously
linked arms to approach the stage. After
graduation we collided cars in the first
car crash for both of us. We decided:
We can't avoid each other, We may as
well marry.

WEDDING CEREMONY:

I tripped over my wedding trail into the
arms of my groom. He caught me, but
his watch became tangled with my veil
which ripped as he pulled himself free.

WEDDING RECEPTION:

A three-hundred and fifty pound football
star, nicknamed Gorilla, grabbed my
groom and threw him into the bass
drum on stage. I ran to the rescue. My
groom was wedged into the drum rim
and needed to be cut out. The Fire
Engines blared. The guests left like rats
fleeing a sinking ship.

DAILY LIFE:

Our families excitedly dispute how we'll
live our lives. As I watch them, I see a
jungle filled with vines from which both
sets of in-laws are flaying over our
affairs with swinging arms grabbing
vines and swooping to the other side.
As I leave the jungle with my children, I
hear a final whoop, whoop, whoop, of
danger screams from the monkeys.

Our girls spit and rear their backs like
cats. Our boys act like dogs jumping
and barking and chasing after them.
The menagerie outside the house is
slightly easier to handle than the one in
the house. Although I'm not sure. The

children have all transformed into leap frogs. I hate frogs.

I'm happy to see my husband return home until he acts as if he's a dancing elephant whose light step on my posies finally saves them from destruction (And him from receiving my wrath.)

I guess I'm the giraffe who has her head high enough above to oversee the happenings.

LIFE EVENTS:

At the funeral parlor, a skull bones and sword rivets my attention. I witness the piracy of one ship falling prey to the clumsy scavenging of pirates. Life is certainly a thriller.

After creating your own unique film or story line, notice that it punctuates an awareness of the difficulties inherent in your marriage. You can recreate the comical aspect, but the facts will remain the same. Hopefully this new perspective will give yourself and your family the energy to organize future scenes with a revised script. Humor can clear the slate.

The use of imagery can be functional. Purchase several dozen colorful balloons. As you blow them up, imagine that your breathe contains all the problems of your life. Now blow that pain into a balloon. When you feel a release of tension in your body, tie the bubble off and and let it float away. Repeat the process as frequently as needed until their is no stress left in your body. Now, enjoy the view; the panorama of colors. (Check first and make certain that there are no ecological laws which would prevent you from following this suggestion.) If there is, then let the balloons float in your room. Kick and destroy the balloons and the negative feelings. With each kick, announce, "I kick out my pain."

New perspectives are important. Take the title of this book for instance, HOW TO TRAIN YOUR HUSBAND TO BECOME AN ADULT. This title implies that the male is lesser than the female. This stance was taken to help women, who grant men privileges with awe struck obedience, i order to view men in a different context. Once a man is no longer a godlike image, the woman can finally reshuffle her attitudes and resolve to treat her man as an adult and expect the same respect in return. The way we view life determines our goals and our outcomes.

The daily routine might be seen as this; Images of two swans who prune each other's wings for a life time. Their offspring is gently pushed back into formation by both parents. A gentle comforting life of sun and showers.

Harmony is stressed. What we envision, so we will fashion into out daily lives. That is done with skills and plans. If you don't have them. Make them. Find them. Locate clear concise messages within yourself; instead of muddied expressions that leaves your husband in a catch 22 situation.

If you want respect in your daily life, decide what respect means to you. An illustration follows:

The husband says: How dare you tell me I shouldn't have purchased a new gulf club. In the next breathe he states: "You snuck behind my back and purchased a baby safety seat."

The wife says: "I'm following your rules. When you tell me in advance that you want new gulf clubs, I'll share my purchases with you. The wife continues: Respect is when the rules for you are the same for me, and vice versa. Moreover your purchase benefited only yourself. Mine could save our child's life and is legally dictated. It's hardly comparable".

It may hurt someone to tell them something they did is now creating resentment towards you, but there are two kinds of hurts. One is a deliberate provocation to wound, and the other is a desire to prevent oneself from being abused. The latter is not aggressive, merely assertive. If one's husband feels threatened by truth, that is a problem he needs to work out with a counselor.

The wife says: I want to leave you. I'm unhappy.

The husband says: It's a bad time for me to hear this. You hurt me.

The wife says: You feel attacked by circumstances. We need to recreate more warm fuzzy feelings so that I'll want to stay. I've lost my cuddle bear.

The husband says: I didn't know you had a toy bear.

The wife says: You were my bear. I miss your comfort. I've been caring for you right along, but I haven't gotten any reciprocation. I'm burning out.

The wife assertively, but kindly tries to express her emotions. The imagery of a cuddle bear can have a prearranged significance for both partners to take time out to listen and comfort each other. Make up other expressions or images that will convey a rapid concept to your partner. It creates a mood recalled from a past glow.

USE IMAGERY TO CHANGE YOUR ATTITUDES:

When life is difficult try unique imagery that you predetermine such as the examples below:

A postal worker found that he had backaches from carrying the mailbag. Since he found the horse a majestic animal I suggested he thought of himself proudly strutting with his load on his back. He did and informed me that the painful condition had ceased. Probably because he was balancing the weight more evenly.

Worried? Let God hold your burdens in a free-floating turtle's shell. Allow them to become one with the inundating waves.

Frightened? Prancing horses might evoke proud, courageous emotions.

Bored with the sameness of lovemaking?: Gorgeous male peacocks

with purple-eye-colors patiently
vibrating conjures up the allurement of
a romantically timed and shared
moment with ones mate.

I was at the airport and had one of
those one half mile jaunts to make in
five minutes to catch the next plane out.
I thought of a jaguar's smooth muscle
tone as it bounds across the prairie. I
emulated it mentally and arrived, on
time, relaxed, and breathing normally.
In the past, without the use of imagery,
I'd arrive stressed and breathless.

Imagery to correct angry reactions; it is
difficult to restrain not lashing back
when no one seems to listen to your
words. Create a new understanding
that eliminates hurts before they begin;
and abruptly stops them before they
start. A discussion of mental imagery
during a peaceful moment that suits
both parties can develop an accord that
endures during more stressful times.

This strategy may be labelled IMAGERY
REPLACEMENT.

It is an agreement to identify certain negative behaviors with hilarious or fanciful concepts in order to replace upsets with comedy or positive thoughts.

For example:

The couple has identified the husband's over reactions to tensions. They developed this story to signal to clam down when when things become heated: A raging bull is plunging at the red cape. Just as the cape is yanked back, the bull charges the red brick wall that is now revealed. The bull knocks himself out. Now when the husband becomes distraught over minor Items, the wife simply says: Raging Bull.

Or the wife might want her husband to understand and acknowledge that his raucous moods frighten her. She might explain that whenever she says, humming bird, that she is identifying her hovering in place to observe what appears dangerous and then zooms away faster than the eye can detect.

Verbalizing the image of a humming bird, gives the man one last imagery to save his marriage before his wife flees.

Besides the story line and imagery suggestions, one can use another formula for comedy.

Utilize your favorite comic show and place yourself into its framework.

For example:

A family show entitled Married With Children points up conflicts on many levels that highlights comic replacement. The absurdity of the show removes it from reality to hilarity. (I am not endorsing it. I am simply using it as an example.) Everyone Loves Raymond demonstrated Raymond utilizing skillful techniques to diffuse his wife's anger or frustration. Many of the reruns of the Bob Cosby's shows utilize the extreme innocence of children manipulating adults like a pro. The comic relief is gentler. Your husband's manifesto to avoid marital efforts may be as innocent as a new born. At least, viewed in this manner renders vindictiveness obsolete. Also seeing him as a child takes his power over you away from him, creating a balance of power. Hopefully women will allow themselves to break down their own resistance to masculine take- over.

Having more control over every situation in life, establishes inner peace and ability to handle whatever comes your way, whether it is your husband, children, or life. Plots seen on TV, illustrate how overload or confusion can be viewed as amusing. In the reruns of My Three Sons: The phone rings, the kids demand dinner, the dog chases the cat throughout the house leaving footprints over the newly plastered tile floor, the workman throws his trowel in frustration through the bathroom window, and the door bell continues ringing; has a crowd roaring. They are laughing because they identify with it. The same situation happens at home and you are beside yourself. When you find yourself on overload, step back and relate to it as a sitcom. The laughter will help you complete the day. You may have to exaggerate the circumstances a bit to create enough whimsy, but usually life is far-out enough. It doesn't need any improving.

Absurdity as either an understatement or an overstatement creates Humor. Take any happenstance and stretch it-as far as you can until it is comic.

If you have frustrating situations similar try novel imagery:

Your husband's parents visit weekly. In letting your husband know how this restricts your privacy you might playfully develop a farce: Dad and Mom have invited the entire family-no matter how distant they are to join us in our bedroom during our lovemaking. The crowd has gotten so large that some family members were pushed out the windows when they attempted to get a breathe of fresh air.

Another imagery helps when he shakes his finger at you and you feel as if you are his child. Now imagine he has shrunk; adjust him mentally to be fifteen months old. Have the child stamp his feet, tell you off, and shake his finger at you. After you have managed your fear, deal with your husband as you would with other adults in your life.

Or mentally strip your hubby of clothes if he denounces you in public. Eliminate a fear that should never be in a marital situation. Create hilarity for yourself or others whenever stress is causing a dysfunction. Don't limit drollness to those times, but include it in those events. In more serious situations where you are feeling helpless because your husband strips you of resources such as a car, money, his time and so forth you might use a paradoxical approach with a playful flair. Coyly say: That's just what I need! More of: less money, less love, less sex, and less of your time. You just made my day! (In wars, the more we know of the enemy, the better equipped we are to win it. The more you are in control of yourself, the better able you are to handle the situation so that the desired outcome is to your liking. Be in control with buffoon relief.

Life can be more mirthful. Happiness lends itself to laughter. However if you see no comedy in something, no amount of explaining will enlighten you.

Take the weather. "You don't want it?"

We'll use it as an example, anyway. If one sees God's tears as rain, one will feel cleansed. God's snow as his blanket, one will feel comforted. God's sun as his soul, one is warmed. God's cyclones, tornadoes, earthquakes, as his upsets, one is amused to learn he has all your imperfections. The above example is an unexpected concept, therefore it is ironic.

Parody can be found in the sacred to the insane to the inane. Mix dissimilar ideas and match them unexpectedly to create humor. Some words have different meanings. Dick and dick. Trick and trick. Both have sexual connotations. Both have innocent meanings. We pun all the time. Use puns to lighten your load when they fit the circumstances.

Use jokes to decrease your tension.

For example:

Lil read aloud from the newspaper Jacks horoscope. You are going to have a romantic evening with candlelight tonight with a Virgo. Virgo was Lil's birth month. Lil looked at her TV couch potato husband and said, "I guess the electric company is turning off the lights without informing us again." Jack said, "Why? Are they out there working again?" "No", Lil said, but that's the only way we'll have a romantic night."

Lil is lightly alluding to a serious problem; her resentment towards Jack's non communicative ways. Hopefully this will create a discussion. Lil needed to request Jack to shut off the TV so they could develop a friendship first, and then become lovers. (After all, its legal. They're married.)

Notice that timing is important. Waiting for an opportune moment or creating such a time will create a better setting for the jesting. It, also, makes a lasting impression that will change the behavior without having to nag.

I used comedic timing effectively when I needed to have my youthful husband mow the lawn. I asked once and he suggested I do it. I stated I wouldn't I had enough to do. We'd purchased a home in the suburbs and the neighbors were complaining about the extremely tall grass.

My husband never noticed. I made no more comments to him about it. One day he entered the kitchen upon his return home from work, ready to eat supper. Lyman said, "Someone must have opened the dog kennel up the street. There are a bunch of dogs in our yard. "I said,"They think it's the woods." Lyman gave me a baffled look, "What are you talking about? We don't have that many trees on our property." I looked him straight in the eye and said, "The grass is so high, they think it's the woods. It was up to your hips as you walked into the house. Didn't you notice?" A strange look crossed his face. He said nothing, but he mowed the lawn before he sat down to dinner. In our entire three decades of marriage he mowed the lawn faithfully every week, and even on the afternoon before his death. Not once did I repeat my request that the lawn be mowed.

Timing and wit is that powerful. My clients report successes of similar nature to me.

CHAPTER 23

BE FIT WITH WIT

(So are we a Frog or Royalty?)

Life should be viewed as a stage. Let's make ours a three ring circus. Fun but organized. Begin by allowing yourself to play. Play inspires creativity. It expands the boundaries of expression. It allows freedom of expression. Did you try developing your own comic script from the preceding chapter's suggestions?

The family members can be the performers. Do you want your play to be a comedy or a tragedy? We feel as though we have no control over life's contents, but we author our text to be whatever we wish it to be. We can make it a comic-tragedy even if life deals a cruel hand.

Ask yourself: (Do I want to remain a Frog?)

1. Do I like being miserable?

2. Can I change the past?

3. Can I change the present?

4. Can I change the future?

5. Would I like to live in peace and harmony with my environment?

Hopefully you responded negatively to numbers one and two and affirmatively to numbers three through five.

The present situations will change when you accept circumstances and ferret out the benefits from them. There is always a reward. Tragedies may be viewed as learning experiences.

For example:

You rollick over yesteryear's events with a comrade, even though they were embarrassing, frustrating, or tragic. What causes them to become the capricious moment for you now?

Time has developed a distance
between the high expectations and the
unfulfilled assumptions that had caused
the old hurts. Time has developed a
distance between the hurts. Now
distance has resolved them. Imagine
your present situation as if you are
viewing life's stage through a time-
telescope. Now put down your
magnifying glass and view the
happenstance at a distance, but see it
in relationship to the other players, the
theme, i.e., the culture, and the
outcome. What is your goal? Happiness
or tragedy?

How can you make your life a comical
play? What makes a good play? A well
thought out script. Life requires the
same reasoned plot. The play-writers
need to extemporaneously fit their
script to develop the theme of
happiness and the goal of peace. You
are the author and the actor. Scribe
your own Broadway production!

What we imagine, we give birth to, and
nurture, until we obtain the outcome.

Picture your problem as if it belonged to a friend of yours. View it as a challenge! You can help yourself to view your life playfully. Now use your own solutions. You are capable of it. You just need to distance yourself from the situation.

We have learned to negatively use imagery all the time. You imagine that your husband will be angry with you if you express your feelings in front of him. You hear every word he says and your response. We subversively undermine our behavior based on our thoughts and then the self-fulfilling prophecy follows exactly as we have imagined.

Reverse the imagery, imagine that your husband is pleased with your utterances because you actively create a teasing light atmosphere. You author your words so that they are cheerfully scintillating.

For example:

The wife is annoyed that the husband is showering first because his toiletry takes less time than hers. She must shower, wash her hair, set it, then apply makeup, get dressed and then find the correct jewelry to match her ensemble. Her husband needs only to shave and shower, put on his suit, tie and tie pin and he's ready.

The wife says, "Why didn't you let me shower before you. Now we are going to be late!"

The husband says, "I'm always wrong no matter what I do!"

The wife may draw back telescopically and see the events, then widen her view to take in the fact that she really could have showered earlier than her husband, but choose not to do so because she didn't feel like rushing. Now her answer takes in this objective perspective and she mockingly teases, "Yes you're always to blame all the time!" She kisses him,... winks and says, "Let's blame you tonight. It'll get me off the hook for making us late."

Her husband picks up the lightness in her voice and responds with, "O.K. I'll tell them it was all my fault that we're late." They both laugh at their private joke, and the hostility deflates.

Here is a second example:

The husband is telling his spouse that she can't go food shopping because it's dark out and he fears she will be mugged. The wife is angry because she's rebelling against her husband's domineering ways. She feels as if he's acting as if he were her father. She will not let him domineer her life; but before she speaks, she explores her husbands motives (which is the micro level). Yes he is trying to control her, but on further consideration she decides that it is because he loves her (which is the exploration of the macro level). Now her light comment is, "Love like yours is hard to come by." She pauses because the punch line has to sink in as a comic approach. "But this is a lifetime prison sentence." She has a twinkle in her eyes as she does a two step out the door, "And I've just escaped!"

In this third situation, the husband is attempting to put his wife down in order that he might feel the bigger/ better person. The husband is stating, "You forgot to sign your pay checks again. How did you think I could cash them?" His first sentence was a fact.

The husband has a valid point, but he was rubbing in the error with his second sentence since the outcome was obvious. His spouse could remind him that he made the same error only the week before when she tried to cash his checks. This is an accounting procedure and must be presented as such or it will be viewed as vindictive. A tit for tat approach is seldom effective in resolving differences.

Exaggeration may be used to effectively point out all the issues generated here. The spouse may roll her eyes flirtatiously, and with a good natured laughter, say, "Whatever would

I do without you? You never have made an error in your life!"

In this fourth situation the male is correct, but he is hitting a sore spot with his wife; her children by a former marriage. Women protectively guard against any possible physical or mental attack that might bring harm to their offspring. The husband (stepfather) states, "You are spoiling Margie by giving her everything she wants."

The wife explores her reasons for siding with her daughter. She recalls that only yesterday she slapped Margie for being disrespectful, but won't allow her husband one word of rebuke. She comprehends that this isn't fair. Her husband's behavior is responsible. She is overprotective with deteriorating results. After evaluating her own motives, the mother remarks, "When you are right, you are right," with a bright smile.

In the fifth example, the husband loudly fusses that he can't find the book on the book shelf. The wife asks, "Did you look on the bookshelf?" He responds, "Yes." Therefore, his wife turns the house upside down, searching for his book, only to find it where it was supposed to be. Her husband had twirled around in the middle of the room as her twelve-year-old would, and declared his impatience, because it's easier to be waited on than actually search. His wife could become furious, or she might say, "I'll find an Aladdin's Lamp you can rub, so that next time your things will appear magically!"

Each of these five examples examine the present behavior in light of past and/or cultural modes that develops new insights in order that the wife can objectify her remarks to decrease tension and resolve conflicts.

Moreover, understanding the elements of comedy, assists one to compose a witty response. Overblown comments again such as the title of this book high lights the issues from the myths.

Here is another demonstration;

Mr. Right has just purchased a Jaguar with the saving that was meant to be a sizable down payment on a house. He has three offspring, a wife, and makes thirty-five thousand per year. Mrs. Right is enraged. She sees her security and their future going down the drain.

Mrs. Right has no trouble identifying the source of the problem. The past and the present are of no aid on this occasion except to fuel more frustration and hostility. Therefore, she needs to gain her mate's attention so that he can become cognizant of his actions before the denial of his responsibilities solidifies. Therefore, the Mrs. Right faces the wall of their apartment and gives full expression to the entire range of her frustrated hostile feelings.

Mr. Right becomes concerned because he believes his wife is flipping out. He states, "Mary, you are screaming at the wall."

Mrs. Right stops, smiles, and says, "The wall will give me just as much satisfaction and security as you are giving me." After she obtains his attention, they can have a serious discussion about the return of a vehicle that they are unable to afford.

Assessing the situation according to the cultural role frames, facilitates identifying enigmas. The historical marital roles are not always readily noticeable.

Take the case of Sally. Sally hired a professional Electrician to put additional outlets in the house. When she attempted to turn on the lights that evening, the entire house blacked out.

Sally's husband, Joe, returned home and blamed her for the black out. Joe said, "Did you check to see if the fuse boxes are turned on?" She said, "Why should I do that? The electrician was just here." She thought: Even if I had remembered, I wouldn't know how to do it.

Joe said, "You're stupid. It's up to you to check the work when it's completed."

The following day the cleaning lady came while Joe was home. The cleaning lady polished the chairs with old English furniture polish. After she left Joe sat down in the captain's chair wearing his clean white shift. He leaned his elbow on the arm rest. As he raised his arm to eat, he noticed that he had a brown stain on his sleeve.

Sally could have called him stupid for not double checking the work, but she realized that his lack of experience with housework and her lack of electrical skills were gender traits encouraged by our culture. Therefore she had taken the step toward removing herself from personalizing Joe's crude remarks by objectifying the situation. Revengeful accusation would create circuitous retaliations.

What should Sally's next step be? How can she create Humor here? Remember that you can't get a play review if no one comes to see the play. So we advertise to get attention. Just as the TV adds create some ludicrous, attention-getting concise slogan, the woman can fashion her add to read in this manner:

Unisex Service person needed for repairs Call Phone #777-7777.

Sally could present this advertisement to Joe for his approval with a comment, "Since, I, as a woman, am dumb electrically, and you, as a male, have no foresight in the ways of housekeeping, I suggest we hire androgynous assistants with gender skills.

What if Joe refuses to acknowledge the similarities of this dissimilar happenstance? After all he probably pointed out that this was not his fault. By default it becomes Sally's duty to remove the furniture polish stain on his shirt unless she speaks up. She might counter with, "You got the stain on you. You get it out!" He responds, "I don't know how to get stains out. That is your job."

"Exactly!" Sally says, then walks away. Timing your responses to create the greatest impact with your words takes patience, but it pays off.

Joe follows her into the next room, "What do you mean exactly?"

"You just proved my point You don't know how to remove stains. You don't think to check the furniture after the cleaning lady has been here, to see if she has completed the job so it won't bleed on our clothes. Housework is considered a female occupation. However when a male job is finished, the female is supposed to realize that the fuse boxes should be checked. Well that's a skill I wasn't expected to learn and I didn't. So we're even. Now let's talk about

educating each other or picking up the slack for gender jobs without demoralizing each other for things that are not our fault, since we are products of our society."

Sally assessed the situation and obtained Joe's attention. (It doesn't have to be an advertisement. A remark, actions, any interesting reaction, may establish his attention. You might engage him by asking for a discussion period without distorting yourself with bizarre reactions!) After Sally has Joe's attention, then she is able to explain and offer solutions for them to discuss. One must dig deeply to find mirth. The last example illustrated both absurdity and unexpected behavior in order to create humor in an explosive situation.

Pleasantry is difficult to develop but keep in mind:

1. Assessing the situation.

2. Creating a time differential in order that you evaluate your priorities from a distant perspective.

3. Utilize the components of exaggeration, such as: absurdities, irony. etc.

4. Contrasting and comparing situations in such a manner that you deliver an unexpected action or comment which will relieve tension and resolve differences.

The above takes practice, but it becomes a fun-filled exercise because it establishes calm where belligerence used to rein. Think of silly, off the wall comments or actions that directly link the action to the problem.

Let's practice a lesson in irony. We will use verbiage to convey a deliberate contrast between the apparent and intended meaning. Your husband has slept all day Saturday as you have washed the floor, shopped for the week's food, put away the items, scrubbed both bathrooms from top to bottom, taken down the curtains throughout the house, washed them plus the windows, and have now begun dinner. Nor does he notice that anything was accomplished while he slept. Therefore, you remark that you have slept all day long and feel very rested. Your husband expresses surprise that he wasn't aware that you were beside him. You remark, "Oh yes, I sleepwalked all day as I (--fill in the blanks with your activities.)

Or one might try a humorous comment with Mr. Late who nonchalantly arrives home several hours after the factory closed. Mrs. reflects out loud, "I was wondering if our house got lost." It's important to get the attention of the person so that there is a discussion pertaining to the dissatisfaction. Repartee may result that will diminish the anger and will cultivate intimacy.

Ask for family participation in playing out a fairy tale that identifies the cause of, or the reactions of both your disappointments, frustrations, expectations, or desires. When your husband growls at you, play the big bad wolf with him and growl back. The absurdity of two adults spontaneously acting as animals in the wild might bring instantaneous laughter.

The wife may feel left out because she no longer is treated romantically. She might dress in rags and request that prince charming rush to save her. This puts the onus in perspective.

Play the three bears who don't want to share their porridge when Dad confiscates all the resources for his play-toys.

Think about what the characters signify. You can utilize the Sesame St. Big Bird, Kermit the Frog, Miss Piggy, and so forth to establish a funny, but pointed reconditioning of old hurts. Make up your own stories based on your life situation. Perhaps these pageants will become an entertaining part of your life. These are similar to the "Imagery Replacements" example in the preceding chapter. For instance: your husband might make fun of your weight, but note that Miss Piggy handles hers with dignity. You might replace the air of confidence by emulating her actions until you wish to create an external difference.

Again, as I stated in the forward, this book is for the normal healthy relationships that will allow a witty approach. Rigid or disturbed personalities may become violent when approached with avant-garde methods because they are unable to cope with creative flexible environments.

Therefore, a humorous approach may be invalid with these types of people.

By now you know that HOW TO TRAIN YOUR HUSBAND is a big lie, a fantasy, a tale. You can only train yourself to become more open, flexible, creative, and humorous in order to try to draw your spouse into the main stream alongside you.

You can give yourself permission to do for yourself, to give yourself options and choices, to communicate effectively, and even humorously. Hopefully that will renovate the relationship.

More than anything else women need to ask themselves, "Is that my problem?" Women tend to possess the need to be the caretaker assuming everyone's responsibilities, and most specifically their husband's concerns. Women can nudge, draw attention to, and create laughter to decrease tension, but they have to stop picking up the thousand pound emotional/loads of other people. Let the men carry their own problems. If they can't do it, then make your decision as to what your options are. Live with them or leave them, but don't fret. Life is too short for that.

Too many women follow this pattern: The saintly wife said to God upon arriving at the Golden Gates of heaven,, "Why did you make my life so difficult?" God gave the wife an amazed look, "Why did you own every problem? Didn't I send you enough challenges?"

I hope the Frog tale awakens
awareness to other means of
communication in order to improve your
life to the stature of Prince and
Princess.

FINI

BIBLIOGRAPHY

Adams Linda/Lenz Elinor: Effectiveness Training For Women., ETW. Calif., NY; Putman Press, 1979.

Albrecht, Ruth.E./Bock, Wilbur E. : Encounter:Love Marriage and Family. Mass; Holbrook Press, Inc., 1975.

Allen Steve:How To Be Funny. NY; Prometheus Books, 1987.

Bach George R./Wyden Peter: The Intimate Enemy:How to Fight Fair In Love And War. NY; Wm. Morrow & Co., 1969.

Benson Herbert:The Relaxation Response. NY; Avon,1975.

Bell Robert R.,Ed.: Studies in Marriage and the Family, 2nd Ed. NY;Thomas Y. Crowell Co., 1968.

Bell Robert R.: Marriage & Family Interaction. NY; Dorsey Press,1975.

Berne Eric: Game People Play. NY; Grove Press,1964.

Blood Bob/Margaret joint authors: Marriage, 3rd Ed.. England, 1962.

Campbell/ Mayer: The Power of Myth. NY; Doubleday, 1988.

Carnes Patrick:The Sexual Addiction. MinnÇ; Compcare Pub.,1983.

Chopra Deepak:The Path To Love. NY; Random House, 1977.

Christensen Harold T./Johnson. Kathryn P.: Marriage And the Family., NY; Ronald Press ., 1971

p. 274 Comparison of three cultural types of husband-wife roles. (Adapted from Kirkpatrick, 1963, pp.168-69).

Cousin Norman: Anatomy of an Illness as Perceived by the Patient. NY; W.W.Norton & Co., 1979. U.S.News And World Report ,What You Believe and Feel Can Have An Effect On Your Health. 1-23-84, pp.61-62.

Dowling Colette:The Cinderella Complex. NY; Summit, 1981.

Erickson Erik,H.:Childhood and Society. NY; W.W. Norton, 1963.

Erickson Erik H. : Identity, Youth & Crisis. NY; W.W. Norton, 1968.

Fawcett Bernadine: Hear My Cry! WVA; University Press,1989.

Freedman Carl:History, Fiction, Film, Television, Myth: The Ideology of M*A*S*H*. The Southern Review, 1990, CBS TV series. Original movie based on Richard Hoo∏ker's book.

French Marilyn:The Women's Room. NY; Summit Books,1977.

Freud Sigmund: The Standard Edition of the Complete Psychological Works of Sigmund Freud, London; Hogarth Press, 1974. Refer to his comments on female hysteria.

Ginott.Haim G.: Between Parent & Teenager. NY; Maxillan, 1969.

Goodhearted, Annette PhD.: Laughter Therapy. She hails from Calif. Appeared at Health/ humor conferences, The

Power of Laughter and Play, sponsored by The Institute for The Advancement of Human Behavior,Stanford Calif.

Gordon Thomas:P.E.T.Parent Effectiveness Training. NY; P.H.Wyden, 1970.

Gray John: Men Are From Mars, Women Are From Venus. NY; Harper Collins,1992.

Grotjahn Martin: Beyond Laughter;Humor and the subconscious. NY; McGraw Hill, 1966.

Hall Calvin,S., & Lindzey Gardner: Theories of Personality, 3rd Ed., NY; Wiley,1978.

Hall Granville Stanley: Youth; Its Education, Regimen and Hygiene,1906. Also was the founder of the American Journal "of Psychology. Hall believed that women were the weaker sex and needed extra rest while at school. His work encompassed the 1800's.

McDonald Paula/Dick: Guilt Free. NY; Grosset & Dunlop.1977.

Maslow Abraham H.: The Power of Self Actualization, Sound Cassette recorded Neat Esalen Institute, 1992.

Maslow Abraham H., Toward a Psychology of Being, 2nd Ed., NY; Van Nostrand,1968.

Moody,Raymond A.,Laugh After Laugh, The Healing Power of Humor . Fla.; Headwaters Press,1979.

Piaget Jean: Judgment & Reasoning In The Child.. England, 1965., The Morale Judgment & Reasoning of The Child. NY: Free Press, 1965.

Restak Richard M.:The Brain. NY;Bantam Books,1984.

Rogers, Carl Ransome; On Becoming a Person. Boston, Houghton Mifflin, 1962.

Rubin Lilian B.: Intimate Strangers. 1983

Rubin Theodore Isaac:Compassion and Self-Hate. NY; David McKay Company, Inc. 1975.

Rubin Theodore Isaac: One On One. NY; Viking Press, 1983.

Rugg Harold: Imaginat"ion. NY; Harper & Row, 1963

Shaywitz Bennet, Shaywitz Sally E. (et.al.): Sex Differences in the Functional Organization of the Brain for Language.Nature, Vol 373, p. 607, 2-16-95. Yale research team illustrates with graphics the electronically monitored subjects' brains responding in different hemispheres to a verbal puzzle.

Siegel Bernie S.: Peace, Love & Healing. NY; Harper & Row.1989.

Siegel Bernie S: Love, Medicine & Miracles. NY; Harper & Row,1986

Simonton, Carl O.: The Healing Journey. NY;Bantam Books, 1992.

Singer Dorothy/ G. Revenson Tracey A. : A Piaget Primer: How a Child Thinks. NY; Plume, 1978.

Spitz A.Rene: The Psychoanalytic
Study of The Child. Vol . I p .53-74, Vol.
II. I pp.113-117. NY, 1945

Smith Manuel J.:When I Say No I Feel
Guilty. NY; Bantam Books,1975.

Spock Benjamin: Baby and Child
Care ,updated NY; Dutton, 1985.
Outlines behaviors in every
developmental stage.

Steiner Claude M. : Scripts People Live.
NY:Random House, Inc.,1974.
The Therapeutic Values of Laughter,
Integrative Psychiatry, Jan. 1985. CBS
series of M*A*S*H*

43894926R00272